The Ford Distinguished Lectures . . . Vol. IV

The Corporation in the Emergent American Society

by

W. Lloyd Warner

University Professor of Social Research,
Michigan State University
and Ford Distinguished Visiting Professor; School of Commerce,
Accounts, and Finance; New York University

HARPER & ROW, PUBLISHERS,
NEW YORK AND EVANSTON

Library of Congress catalog card number: 62-9916

TO
Chester I. Barnard

Contents

Charts and Tables

Foreword

THROUGH the Ford Distinguished Visiting Professorship, which was made possible by a grant from the Ford Foundation for the purpose of bringing to the School of Commerce outstanding educators from American and overseas universities, the School has had the privilege, in previous years, of hearing such eminent men as Sir Noel Hall, Dr. Ordway Tead, and Professor Herbert A. Simon.

The School was indeed fortunate during the spring of 1961 in having Professor W. Lloyd Warner, University Professor of Social Research, Michigan State University, deliver, on April 13, 20, and 27, three public lectures on the general topic, "The Corporation in the American Community," now published under the title of *The Corporation in the Emergent American Society*. There is no one in America who is better qualified to discuss this subject than Professor Warner, an eminent sociologist and anthropologist.

Educated at the University of California and Harvard University, Professor Warner has spent the last twenty-five years studying American communities, with special emphasis on their social structure and symbolic behavior. This study has involved research in New England, the Deep South, the Middle West, and the Far West. Currently he is conducting research for a study of large-scale organizations in American communities and in American society as a whole, under a grant from the Carnegie Corporation of New York. The present lectures are partly an outgrowth of this research as well as the fruition of his other monumental studies.

Professor Warner is the author or co-author of fifteen books in the area of the social sciences, including *The Yankee City Series; American Life, Dream and Reality; Big Business Leaders in America;*

Occupational Mobility in American Business and Industry; The Living and the Dead; and *Industrial Man.* Each of these original studies —and others as well—has stamped him as one of the great research anthropologists and sociologists of our time.

The approach to the study of the corporation takes many forms— financial, legal, organizational, functional, and human—to mention a few. Professor Warner has added new dimensions by dealing with the corporation from an anthropological point of view. His contribution in these lectures is an important addition to the literature.

We at the School of Commerce believe that the proper study of business and its administration calls for the contributions of men in the many academic disciplines, because each contribution enables the student of business to understand better the many facets of a dominant institution in American life. Greater knowledge and understanding of business, which are so essential for the future of America, will come about when eminent social and behavioral scientists, such as Professor Warner, also focus their unusual abilities on this important subject. The School of Commerce is honored to have had the privilege of having him as Ford Distinguished Visiting Professor and of publishing his lectures.

THOMAS L. NORTON, Dean
School of Commerce, Accounts,
and Finance
New York University

Acknowledgments

THIS book is based on three lectures I gave in the spring of 1961 as Ford Distinguished Visiting Professor at the School of Commerce, Accounts, and Finance of New York University. Essentially, the lectures and chapters are similar; the presentation now is for reading, rather than listening.

The content is from previous research and from field studies now being pursued. Under the guidance of colleagues and myself, and financed by the generosity of the Carnegie Corporation, a nationwide investigation of large-scale complex organizations and the emergent society is under way. Detailed research publications are planned; at that time I shall thank others for use of their research and publications. In this little book, for simplicity and easy reading, I have eliminated all footnotes but one and all other apparatus of scientific publication.

For previous publications on which much of the book is founded the five volumes of the *Yankee City Series* (Yale University Press), two volumes on big-business leaders by Dr. James Abegglen and myself—*Big Business Leaders in America* (Harper & Brothers) and *Occupational Mobility in American Business and Industry* (University of Minnesota Press)—as well as *Industrial Man,* which I edited with Norman Martin (Harper), should be consulted.

I wish to thank Harper & Brothers, particularly my friend and colleague, Dr. Ordway Tead, for permission to use materials for this present volume. I am also indebted to the Yale University Press and the University of Chicago Press for use of short pieces of evidence from my previous writings to support some of the argument of this book.

Above all I want to thank Professor Thomas L. Norton, Dean of the School of Commerce, Accounts, and Finance at New York University, for his invitation to give the lectureship and for his, and his colleagues', warm and generous hospitality to my wife and me during our stay in New York City.

I wish to thank my colleague and friend, Professor Norman Martin, of New York University, for use of certain research evidence discussed in these pages. I would also like to thank Assistant Dean Harry Kelly and Miss Patricia Coleman of New York University, and many others of that institution, for their many kindnesses.

I am deeply indebted to my friend and colleague, John Honey, of the Institute of Public Administration. His intellectual and spiritual affirmation aided me greatly in undertaking these lectures.

I am honored to have permission to dedicate this small book to that very great man, Chester I. Barnard, who, in my opinion, knows more about great corporations, large-scale organizations and, for that matter, the emergent society itself than anyone now alive.

POSTSCRIPT

As indicated, the previous paragraph and the dedication were written before Mr. Barnard's recent death. Since copy was still in typescript when he died, I could have changed the form of the dedication. I did not because the full significance of the dedication lies in the fact that he was then alive. It offers one small expression of the deep admiration that those in the social sciences, business, government, and civic life felt and will always feel for this great man.

Introduction

THE story about communities, corporations, and the emergent American society told in this small book is a large and complex one. Despite its scope and many themes I have chosen to tell it briefly and simply. No more than illustrative evidence is presented; detail, citation, and proof are left largely to other publications. Research now in progress continues to probe the scientific problems and test the hypotheses here presented.

It is contended that local communities in America have lost much of their previous autonomy, but this loss is no more than one movement in a larger transition, an emergent process, in which the more significant development is the coming into being of a great society. The whole American society is rapidly growing into one *primary* community, in which corporations along with other complex hierarchical structures play their significant and necessary roles. Change is built into the very nature of this social system, most innovations originating from within, not from without; yet to maintain order and still change, this society continuously incorporates its persistent past into its moving future.

As part of this process the rationality of science and technology seeps through the values, beliefs, and practices of the national society, its several parts, and many institutions. Meanwhile, opposing non-rational[1] moral values grow, expand, and flow through public opinion, law, government, and other institutions to lodge more and more firmly at the national level. Here, the secular part of the moral order, through the instruments of federal law and its agencies and through the reinforcements of national opinion and its moral values,

[1] "Non-rational beliefs and values are those which arise out of the basic individual and cultural assumptions—they supply the solid core of mental and emotional life—they are not irrational or maladaptive—but they do not have their source in [man's] rational processes" (*The Living and the Dead,* Yale University Press, 1959, p. 5).

confronts the non-moral demands of technology, science, and the market place. Corporate hierarchies, now located more often in a few metropolitan economic centers, and big government, centered in one political metropolis, along with other great complex organizations, such as the church, the school, and associations, are themselves products of this same emergent process. They are necessary parts of the structure and growth of the great primary American community.

The once locally owned corporate enterprises of owners and managers and workers and the predominantly autonomous local communities were functionally contained and mutually supportive. The church congregations and their Sunday meetings, the local government and its town meetings, the associations and the weekly lodge nights—all of these and many others were once the institutions and assemblages which embodied the powerful autonomy of the local community.

Such institutions and their assemblages performed local tasks and assumed local duties. Their members sought and received rewards, which were bestowed by the institutions that composed the web of community relations. Assemblages most often had the power of decision within the body of collective members. Large corporations which spread nationwide did exist; the federal and state governments did function; some churches did possess national and international ecclesiastical hierarchies; yet, even so, the self-containment of communities and the accent on local autonomy were strong and powerfully felt by all (as symbolized, for example, in their feelings about "my home town"). These local institutions and assemblies still exist, and many are still important, but their dependence on the national community steadily is felt.

Today, the predominant and most characteristic institutions are complex, hierarchical, and spread far beyond the boundaries of any one simple community. The vast growth of church organizations, ecumenical movements, civic, professional, occupational, philanthropic, and other types of association and the rise to dominance of the great corporations, as well as the development of big government and of big national unions among the workers, all provide ample testimony about the formation of the hard scaffolding of the elaborate structure of a national community. The state and municipal governments do possess power; yet, increasingly, ultimate power and moral authority and its sanctioning are located in Washington. There are tens of thousands of local business enterprises, local unions, local philanthropies, local associations all viable and significant; yet for them the accent and significance of today's social order are increasingly national (and for certain purposes international) rather than local and parochial.

To talk about the corporation and the American community, we must talk about local communities but also view them as integral parts of the larger moral order of the emergent national community. To discuss the relations of the family and the corporation, of government and the corporation, of the school and church and the corporation, one must see these institutions not only in their localities but also as parts of the developing great society. To understand persons and individuals in contemporary society they, too, as psychic entities, living and being formed in this emergent community, must be observed and interpreted as integral parts of the process itself. All of these and similar problems are accepted as parts of what we need to understand and say in our examination of the modern corporation in the contemporary American community.

The unfolding of the great corporate hierarchies allied with the development of the superrational and scientific technology can be observed and given significance. The development of big government, opposed to the big corporate structures, is important to understand and make sense of; but these are only the present products of an emergent process that moves through and beyond us. To know what corporations and communities are, to understand big government and big corporations as well as other great complex hierarchies, such as big unions, big education, and for that matter, big churches, we must know what they are as integral parts of the emergent future of our social structure and symbolic life. In this process heterogeneity, variation, and diversity expand, yet yield themselves partly to the counter-movements of homogeneity and tradition. The thrust of innovation pushes forward against the hard but yielding demands of tradition and the past. Thrust and withdrawal, movement and counter-movement, expansion and contraction, transition and persistence, inertia and at times violent action—all these merge and blend, oppose and conflict as identifiable parts of the movements of the great society. The nature of the process is the nature of the emergent American structure; the one is the other.

The first part, "The Corporation, the Community, and the Emergent Process," examines the emergent process, first viewing the loss of local-community autonomy. (Here extensive quotation for its own special significance is given from the research on Yankee City in the 1930's and 1940's as reported on at that time. The few references, explanations, and other acknowledgments to publishers are placed in the Acknowledgments). The spread of corporate hierarchies, big unions, and other institutions beyond local boundaries, through the nation, and up the expanding corporate hierarchy away from small cities to metropolitan headquarters is also reported on. The processes and significance of emergent change in communities and throughout the American society where the corporation has its being are studied and interpreted.

The next, "Big Corporations and Big Government in the Great Society," reports on the changing corporation and the evolving society under the conditions previously described. To interpret some of the restraints on potential innovation and the pressures on tenacious tradition (some having to do with the corporation and the American community) the peculiar political processes in the dual-party system which operate to produce the larger moral and legal structure of the great society are examined.

The last part, "Autonomous Man and the Corporate Process," with more evidence supplied than in the first two, studies some of the popular myths about organization men. The personalities of big business men are analyzed and the mental and moral demands made on them by their high status in the management hierarchies are reported. The two—the personalities of corporation managers and the job status of higher management—are compared, the significance of their compatibility discussed, and conclusions reached.

Thus corporation, community, society, and the personalities who are members of these collectivities are conceptualized and interpreted as significant expressions of the emergent process of the great society.

The Corporation in the Emergent American Society

The Corporation, the Community, and the Emergent Process

CORPORATION, COMMUNITY, AND THE GREAT SOCIETY

ALL Americans know well and feel deeply that they live in a fluid world of change. Indeed, not only do we consciously understand that all parts of our entire society change, but we also sense deep within ourselves the emotional impact of the changing meanings and values that often rise out of our most private selves to confront and plague us. We do so not only because of the advance of age and the passage of time but, in ways far beyond our present comprehension, because we are integral parts of a vast social process that in its transitions and fulfillments absorbs all our public and private lives.

Corporations and local communities in America, as everyone knows, also change swiftly and rapidly. Today they are not what they were yesterday. Tomorrow they will not be what they now are. The structure and functions of the great corporations and the large and small communities and the behavior of those who occupy them are clearly different from what they were in that chronologically near but socially distant past, the First World War. Given the powerful thrust of our society toward the future as it yields to the urgent demands of tomorrow, it seems sure that our present cultural world will be so drastically changed, redefined, and revaluated that to those living at the beginning of the next century our present community life, our corporations, and we ourselves will appear to them as remote, and endowed with significances we would fail to understand.

The transformation of the mental, moral, and technical life of corporate enterprises and their almost revolutionary realignments, and the concentrations of American populations in the space and time

1

of a comparatively few metropolitan communities, now distributed north to south and from the Atlantic to the Pacific, have their own separate histories and significances. These are important and must be understood. But the combined influences of each on the other, corporation on community and community on corporation, are many times more important than the simple arithmetic their combination first indicates. When the developing structures and expanding functions of corporations, the transformations of the older urban forms, and the appearance of innovations in the collective life of our communities are viewed together and understood as a single temporal process they, corporation and community, constitute an even greater significant segment of the social realities of America. The nature and meaning of this process will be discussed.

However, when the combined processes of community and corporate transitions are seen as integral parts of the evolving American society, where church, school, family, and other groups move forward, too, and change their being, the nature of the total process seems possible to understand and to be of incalculable importance scientifically and practically. To confront the smaller task and properly study community and corporation we must also take on the burden of the larger one. We shall view the combined worlds of the corporation and the community in the changing universe of the American society.

The primary tasks of these three chapters, then, are to present and discuss certain propositions about the nature and direction of our emergent social life and about corporation and community developments as they evolve in the larger flow of the great society. Since much of what I shall say comes from my long interest in, and practice of, empirical research on the community, the corporation, and the larger society, most statements are founded on evidence from large and small American communities, including towns, cities, and now metropolitan agglomerations such as Kansas City and Chicago. They are founded, too, on research on the executive careers and corporate behavior of several thousand leaders of our largest corporations and on a more recently completed study of the military and civilian executives of the federal government. What is written also relies on a large research project now under way on corporations and other large-scale organizations and on what I shall call here "the emergent society."

The emphasis, then, will be primarily upon a particular kind of time change that I believe is a necessary and most important part of our social system and of the personalities of those who live in this system. I will be concerned with examining the nature of the emergent processes through which the total American society—its corporations and communities and the individuals in them—evolve to become something more than they now are and something different from what they once were.

To anticipate full discussion of the concept of emergent and say briefly what is meant by the emergent American society: I believe that the nature of our collectivity is such that change is built into it and is an essential part of it; that to be what it is at any one moment in time, this society must continually change and become something else. The processes of change are such that, while the forms of the past are being absorbed into the present and losing their identities, the present ones, re-formed by the future, are becoming something different from what they now are.

In such an emergent process, the past influences the present; and the processes that timewise become the events of the future are already present and, operating there, make their significance felt today before tomorrow's world takes over. Quite literally these activities go on now in the bodies of each of us.

Order is maintained and chaos avoided in our complex society by the holding influences of the comparatively homogeneous world of the traditional past on the increasing heterogeneity expressed in the innovations and experimentations of the evolving future. Heterogeneity, nevertheless, grows and expands but always under effective control. In this world of emergent change all generations are involved in transition. The basic relations of older and younger generations characteristic of all former societies are no longer entirely true; the young not only learn from the old, but the old, to survive, must necessarily learn from the young. All human organisms are involved in this emergent process. Their personalities must be such that to retain their hold on social reality and possibly on their own psychic reality they must continue to learn and unlearn so that they can learn again.

There are several visible and observable massive processes operating in the major areas of American behavior that are part of the emergence of the great society. They can be stated as simple, descriptive, testable propositions on which the inferences I have made about the emergent society can be safely founded. They are:

1. That, following the great migrations of the Nineteenth Century which ended the western frontier, the populations of America have continued to grow and spread throughout all regions of the country. But the ratio of growth of great metropolitan centers has increased and the emphasis upon them as collective habitats of the multitude has accelerated and, through time, increased greatly. These fluid collective agglomerates are the physical realities that symbolize and embody the emergent social process.

2. That the simple economic and other social structures, including corporations, the church, government, education, and associations, once characteristically local, are becoming increasingly complex, large-scale, hierarchical and, often, national or international organizations.

3. That the headquarters of corporations and other large institutions and the high places of decision of all these complex organizations are increasingly centered in a few great metropolises; the decisions made there are such that they are usually national in their extension, complexity, and significance. Thus, the movement of population, the elaboration of the economic and technological structure and of other large-scale organizations, synchronize and join together as parts of the emergent process.

4. That the value and belief systems are increasingly rational, secular, and technological.

5. That the non-rational beliefs of the moral order grow too, nurtured primarily by the family and our experiences in the family; maintained at the national level, they expand and assume new importance.

6. That public opinion structured by political parties helps change the locus of public moral action and sanction from local to national levels; thus it innovates, but the effect generally of the influence of

political parties on political and moral opinion is to maintain traditional values.

7. That the counterforces of traditional homogeneity so operate that many of the older forms of our sacred symbolic life are being reconstituted by movements occurring in and out of the church.

8. That, given the needs of a fluid and flexible society, fixed status is no longer adaptive, creates conflict, and consequently is rapidly changing toward open status, where there is greater freedom for the individual and his family to move unfettered and thus be available for use in a changing world. All the evidence of our research suggests that color caste, closed systems of class, and other forms of rank that permanently fix the place of an individual and his family cannot continue to survive.

9. That education, particularly higher education, has become the great transformer. To its institutions and processes has been delegated the responsibility not only of generating the new ideas of the developing age but of training every variety of human talent to the point that, increasingly, education in the life span of an individual begins in the nursery school and extends, through "continuing education," throughout his life. In our society the educational structure has now spread from the local communities through the state colleges; now, too, the national government and other organizations are influential in determining local decisions.

10. That, related to these changes in our values, beliefs, and behavior, is the rapid development of an elaborate national apparatus of government, of regulatory departments and agencies, that increasingly supports and sanctions the new over-all national morality (now leaving the autonomous local communities to be re-formed in Washington). The new governmental structures and behavior counterbalance this removal of economic and social power from the local communities.

11. That all this is part of the emergent process of the great society. Whether what is happening is good or bad or neither, it is not my purpose as a social scientist to say, but rather it is my task to make sense of it and communicate what the evidence indicates.

A few fundamental questions guide the larger design of my inquiry: What are the processes operating within the moral, technical, and belief systems of corporations and other types of large-scale organizations, including educational, ecclesiastical, and political, which innovate the new, reform the old, and incorporate each into the further emergence of large-scale organizations throughout the United States?

In what directions are local communities, metropolitan agglomerates, market towns, and others in our society moving? And more broadly, as the past moves through the present into the future, in what direction is our total society evolving?

How are such local collectivities, corporations, and other organizations influenced by the emergent processes of the great society?

What are the meanings of these basic questions about the society for understanding individual behavior in America?

To develop the argument about the emergent nature of the changing community and the corporation's relations in the evolving society I shall now turn to our earlier study of the corporation and community in Yankee City. Then, through use of recent empirical research, I shall follow the development of those same corporations into great complex structures as they spread out into the expanding corporate structure of the American society. Once this is done, I shall inspect the results of our study of the behavior of corporate and federal executives throughout the United States. I shall draw certain limited conclusions about corporation and community and then turn again to the larger meaning of the community and corporation as viewed in the emergent process of the great society.

THE EXPANDING CORPORATION IN THE DIMINISHING
LOCAL COMMUNITY

The research on Yankee City, conducted in the early 1930's, first brought some of these factors in the changing American corporate structure and community life into my understanding, particularly the emergent process which interrelates changes in the social and status structures with the technology. The later study, in the 1950's, of several thousand American leaders of big business broadened my view of what was taking place in other communities in the United States. My present research enables me to continue examining the elaboration of these great corporate enterprises.

From a simple and undifferentiated society there developed in

Yankee City the type of economic life which histories of New England have made familiar. During the era of shipbuilding, shipping, and fishing, a great number of handicrafts developed. These included such primary industries as wood-carving, cordage-making, blacksmithing, and sail-making. However, the most important industry, in view of its later development, was the manufacture of shoes.

During the research in Yankee City, a systematic study was made of shoemaking. Part of the study consisted of going back through the records, making use of other studies of the shoe industry generally, to understand some of the changes in direction of the industry itself. We soon learned that we were dealing with not one history of the shoe industry, but several. We were able to trace at least six histories. On Figure I they are spread across the page from left to right, beginning with "Technology" and ending with the "Structure of Relations." The histories of each run from the early beginnings found at the bottom of the page up through other phases to "Today and tomorrow." We could conveniently divide the technological history of Yankee City's shoe industry into five phases. At least two important stories are to be found in the technological history. The tools changed from a few basic ones, entirely hand used, to machines and assembly lines; and the product from a single pair of shoes to tens of thousands in mass production.

The changes in the form of the division of labor are another story of importance. In the beginning, the family made its own shoes, or a high-skilled artisan, the cobbler, made shoes for the family. In time, several families divided the high-skilled jobs among themselves; and later, one man assigned the skilled jobs to a few men and their families. Ultimately, a central factory developed, and the jobs were divided into a large number, systematized and low-skilled. The history of ownership and control is correlated with the changes in the division of labor. In early days, tools, skills, and materials were owned by the family; eventually, the materials were supplied by the owner-manager, and soon the tools and machines, also. The sequence of development of producer-consumer relations tells a similar story. The family produced and consumed its shoes all within the circle of its simple unit; then the local community was the consumer-producer unit; and ultimately, the market became national and even world-

FIGURE I CORPORATION, COMMUNITY, AND THE EMERGENT SOCIETY

	Technology	Form of Division of Labor	Form of Ownership and Control	Producer-Consumer Relations	Worker Relations	Structure of Relations
V Today and tomorrow	Increasing automation, hand and white collar	Low-skilled jobs	Ownership increasingly *remote*	Large chain stores dominant	Consolidation of union strength	National and international corporate structure
IV 1920–1945	*Machine tools:* mass production, assembly line methods	Nearly all jobs low-skilled; a very large number of routinized jobs	*Outside* ownership and control of the factory (tools leased)	Very few retail outlets; factory merely one source of supply for a chain of shoe stores	Rise of industrial unions, state supervised—no (or weak) unions	Center of dominance: New York and Washington. Very complex financial producer and retail structure. Local factory not important in it
III Late intermediate period (approximately to World War I)	*Machine tools:* machines predominate; beginning of mass production through use of the machine (McKay)	Central factory with machines; still high degree of skill in many jobs	First small-scale; later, large *local* men of wealth own or lease the tools, and machines	National market and local capitalist; many outlets	Craft and apprenticeship (St. Crispin's Union)	Center of dominance is local factory; complex hierarchy in local factory system
II Early intermediate period (approximately to the Civil War)	*Machine tools:* few machines, first application (Elias Howe, etc.)	One man assigns highly skilled jobs to few men; highly skilled craftsmen ("letting-out" system)	Small, locally controlled manufacturers; tools still owned by workers, materials by capitalist; market controlled by "owner"	Owner and salesmen to the consumer regional market	Informal, apprenticeship, and craft relations	Economic only; no longer kinship; worker subordinate to manager

	Tools	Skills / Specialization	Control	Market	Labor relations	Economic character
	Hand tools increasing specialization and accumulation of hand tools	Specialization among several families; a few highly skilled jobs	*Local control:* not all shoemakers need own all tools; beginning of specialization	Local buyer from several producer families sells products (no central factory)	Kinship and neighbors among workers	Semi-economic, but also kinship and neighborliness
I The beginning (early 1600's)	*Hand tools* few, basic, and simple	All productive skills in the family, including making of shoes; a few cobblers for the local market	*Local control:* skills, tools, and materials owned and controlled by each family; or by the local cobbler	The family produces and consumes shoes and most other products	Largely family relations among workers	Very simple non-economic; the immediate family

wide. Worker relations changed from those based on kinship and family ties to those based on occupations, where apprenticeship and craftsmanship relations were superseded and the individual unit became dominant in organizing the affairs of the workers. The structure of economic relations changed from the immediate family into a local hierarchy; and the locally owned corporation, into a vast, complex national hierarchy, owned, managed, and dominated by persons and organizations located in New York City.

In the third phase, a new economic role appears, and an older one begins to take on new form and assume a new place in the community. The capitalist is born, and during the several periods which follow he develops into full maturity. Meanwhile, the worker loses control of his time and skills and becomes subordinate in a *local hierarchy*. There are, thus, distinct and opposing forces set up in the shoemaking system. What is good for one is not necessarily good for the other, but the interdependence of the two opposing forces is still very intimate, powerful, and highly necessary. The tools, the skills, and the places of manufacture belong to the worker; but the materials, the place of assembly, and the market are now possessed by the local owner and manager.

In the fourth period, full capitalism has been achieved; the manufacturer is now the owner of the tools, the machines, and the industrial plant; he controls the market. The capitalist has become the supercapitalist; the workers have forgotten their pride in their separate crafts, dismissed the small differences among themselves, and united in one industrial union with tens and hundreds of thousands of workers throughout the country, combining their strength within a hierarchy of their own to assert their interests against management.

In the fifth and present period automation has begun in the technology but has not developed as rapidly as it has in other industries; the jobs are still low-skilled, ownership is further removed and distant from the local community, and the center of dominance and the place of decision are elsewhere, in a great metropolis. In brief, the complex large-scale organizations have tied Yankee City and many other communities that once were local and autonomous into the larger structure of the great national society. Now the principal location of economic power and decision is New York. The regulatory agencies, anti-trust suits, and Supreme Court decisions take the managers and union officials to Washington. Great trade and other associations are often located there, too.

The federal government, by the emergence of moral opinion and national government sanction, has taken over part of what was once the domain of private business and, by regulation and the force of public opinion, has greatly limited the area of free choice for the local communities. The local men of top management now feel the loss of power and freedom of action, which has been further limited by the great unions.

Thus, two fundamental changes have been occurring concomitantly in recent years in the social organization of Yankee City shoe factories. The first is the extension of the hierarchy upward and out of Yankee City through the expansion of huge corporate enterprises in hundreds of communities throughout the United States and the establishment of central offices in distant large cities. The second is the expansion of the structure outward from Yankee City and other towns and cities through the growth of manufacturers' associations and labor unions, also with metropolitan headquarters and with units in many other shoemaking communities throughout the United States. Both the vertical and horizontal extensions have gone on concurrently, each reacting upon the other; both decrease Yankee City's and other communities' control over their factories by subjecting the local corporations, or segments, to more and more control from outside. Power, money, and prestige have flowed up and out from the small city to the great economic metropolises of big business and the great political metropolis of big government.

Meanwhile, the national trade associations of private enterprises, by developing agreements among business competitors which increasingly narrow the area of competition and regulate and restrain the freedom of each of the members, further constrict the local managers' freedom, indicating that the internal organization of business is undergoing changes which are decreasing free enterprise. The so-called free-contract transaction once characteristic of the relations of labor and management in the local community, in which the local individual worker agreed to sell his services for a given wage to a local entrepreneur, has largely vanished. The concept of the "free contract," when exercised by management, was a powerful protector of the economic position of the upper-middle and upper classes and helped control the actions and demands of the lower-class workers. The central government, with new moral authority, now defines the minimum wage; social security as well as other legislative stipulations make the "free contract" less important in the field of labor-management relations.

The Yankee City research concluded that the segmentation of the daily life of the American community and its increasing complexity, accompanied by a corresponding movement to reclassify the social diversities into larger and larger comprehensive social units, have resulted in "great holding companies and gigantic cartels which relate and integrate myriads of diverse smaller units into common corporate enterprises." Meanwhile, the control over these great structures moves steadily up an ever-extended hierarchy into the hands of a smaller and smaller number of powerful men. In the area of government, local grass-root activities become more diverse and more specialized, while the larger political units at higher levels continue to absorb power and control. Power inevitably moves into the upper reaches of the governmental ladder in Washington.

The functions and autonomy of the multitude of local communities throughout the United States diminish radically. Almost all primary interaction used to take place in towns and cities, where face-to-face relations characterized the group life of men and women. At the present time, with the emergence of the great complex organizations that enter all parts of our lives, technological, moral, and sacred, a larger national community has come into being, where direct action, communication, and face-to-face relations now occur.

THE GREAT SOCIETY AND LARGE-SCALE ORGANIZATIONS

The recent developments of the hierarchical and aristocratic structure of corporations and the concentration of economic and social power as well as prestige at the upper reaches have been researched by many varieties of scholars. The corporate hierarchy must be seen comparatively as only one among many kinds of hierarchies. All the older formal groupings, the family excepted, have developed elaborate hierarchies that now spread throughout the national society; the innumerable activities of our many local communities and many of the actions of all our people thus become part of the great society. All these big corporations, big governments, big churches, big unions, and big associations, particularly at the higher levels, are interrelated and in mutual influence.

Each of these great organizations is faced with the problem of relating its order to the larger society, which is also increasing in complexity and heterogeneity. Each "feels" the influence of the others, sometimes as restraint of the amount of change that might have taken place if the organization itself only were concerned. Sometimes, when a hierarchy directly or indirectly feels the radical social changes that occur in one or more of the others, it becomes necessary for it to make radical changes also. The ecumenical movements within the Protestant churches and their efforts to organize themselves into larger orders to be more effective in handling the complex social and spiritual problems created by the emergence of the great society are examples of this kind of influence.

As these great hierarchies expand in size, in complexity, and in heterogeneity, they also extend territorially and in social space. More and more of the local communities and their populations are involved in the developments of these tremendous hierarchies. Meanwhile, the social institutions, in which the hierarchies expand, become increasingly integrated parts of the local communities and are related beyond each to a greater and greater diversity and variety of institutions, people, and subcultures throughout America. As they grow and develop, the fifty states are rapidly becoming one community; in any study of community, corporation, and other large-scale organizations, one must be aware of these facts.

Figure II shows only four major types of complex organization: corporations, big government, ecclesiastical, and big education. Others could be added. The brackets at each side of the chart enclosing the entirety refer to the surrounding society in which the several types of hierarchies operate. It will be noted that interconnected circles are enclosed within rectangles, signifying segmentary hierarchies with several levels. Below each type are the numbers, 1, 2, 3; the number 4 connects the first three.

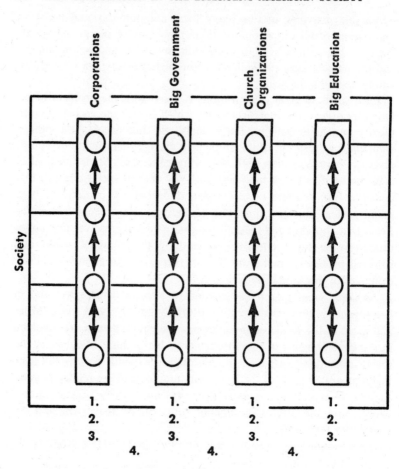

FIGURE II   THE SOCIAL COMPOSITION OF THE HIERARCHIES OF
LARGE-SCALE ORGANIZATIONS

1. Ruled behavior in a hierarchical system.
2. Mental constructs in, and passing among, the statuses of large-scale organizations.
3. Technical knowledge, skills, and machines in change.
4. Relations of 1, 2, and 3 to each other.

Number 1 at the base of each of the several types of hierarchy refers to the legend at the bottom of the chart, "Ruled behavior in a hierarchical system," indicating that each hierarchy is organized, and is being organized, into a system of interrelated statuses and that all of them are ordered by rules and values that operate as part of the hierarchical order. Number 2 refers to the "mental constructs in, and passing among, the statuses of large-scale organizations," whether they be economic, political, ecclesiastical, or academic. As the legend indicates, number 3 refers to the "technical knowledge, skills, and machines" that are part of some of the positions that make up an hierarchical order. Obviously, technical knowledge operates at all levels of the hierarchy, as do some of the skills, but some function only at the lower levels of particular hierarchies. Finally, number 4 indicates that the hierarchies of ruled behavior, mental contructs, and technical knowledge are related to each other at all levels and among the statuses of all organizations.

The horizontal lines, of course, point out that all types of hierarchies are interrelated and are parts of the total American system.

A great primary society is now in being. The many local groups are still important and still necessary parts of our social apparatus, but, instead of having only their own kind of autonomy, they now are integral parts of the larger American, not to say world, social systems. The changes occurring have developed a great society which continues to emerge and become something more than what it now is. Covariantly changing with the structure of this great society is the development of corporate structures, other large-scale organizations, and new ways of thinking and symbol systems which relate men more effectively across diverse regions and diverse divisions of labor.

The evolution of this new world of increasing diversity necessarily means the development of great organizations to relate effectively and coherently all men in the great society, so that they can behave with order and efficiency to get the new, more advanced, and productive social labor done, the work being not only the labor of our economic institutions, but all the social activities of the society itself. Only within this framework can we understand the men and institutions of the large-scale, complex groups that comprise our economic, political, civic, ecclesiastical, and other parts of the American social structure.

Dr. James Abbeglen's and my study, in 1952, of the careers of over eight thousand leaders of the largest corporations, in all types of business enterprise in the United States, brought out two very important bodies of evidence for the present thesis on the emergence of the great society (see Acknowledgments). One of the most general conclusions of the research, which studied father's occupation, education, and territorial origin, was that, at the high managerial levels, in the broadest sense American society is not becoming more caste-like; recruitment of business leaders from the bottom is taking place now and seems to be increasing. Mobility to the top is not decreasing; in fact, for at least the last quarter century, it has been increasing.

The evidence shows that our society is more flexible than it was; more men and their families are in social motion; pessimism about decreased flexibility and mobility is not warranted. Men move up from all levels from communities all over the United States. Most remain in a very few corporations, but they move up within them.

Careers of the big business leaders were studied from the time they first entered a job until they were interviewed, around the age of fifty-three-odd years. This inquiry was also pursued to determine how much circulation there is throughout the United States, from region to region, from small town to large town, and from large city to small town. Only 40 per cent of the business elite are now located in the same state in which they were born, and many of these men have moved from farms and small towns to the great cities. A high rate of territorial mobility characterizes this group of men. Over half of those born in large cities are now located in the same state in which they were born. On the other hand, over half of the men born in the smaller towns (population 2,500 to 25,000) have moved out of the region in which they were born. It may be inferred that a major force in their territorial mobility is the need to move to larger cities to conduct a business career.

The movement of men and their families from community to community is orderly and organized. The daily and hourly communication among those in the same and different corporations is not community-bound but national, and all of it organized largely by the force not only of the great corporate complexes but of other kinds of large-scale organizations in this country. The decisions made at corporate headquarters, mostly in the great economic metropolises, or in the political metropolis of Washington and, occasionally, in state capitals, affect the interrelated complexes of communities and corporations in such a way that they are rapidly merging into what I have called "the great society."

THE EMERGENT PROCESS AND ITS FUTURE DIRECTIONS

Now, once again, we are ready to ask, "What do we mean by an emergent society?" To answer, we must first ask a more specific question: What do we mean by society? Then we can turn to the more important operative question for us: What do we mean by emergent?

As conceived here, the American society is a vast interconnected set of primary relations composed of constituent parts, the whole being a social system. The constituent parts of the structural form of our life are the interrelated social positions which order all the activities of those in the system; the technology which instrumentalizes the system and adapts the whole society to nature; and the symbols, beliefs, and values of the social system, including the conscious and unconscious dealings, the rational and non-rational principles, which motivate and determine the behavior of those involved in the American social system.

All of the parts of this society, we can now say, are emergent and changing, each within itself, each to the other, and each within the total system which is the larger American society.

The increasing application of technical, scientific, and rational knowledge and the skillful use of tools and machines to provide for the material needs of the populace, this technological subsystem, controls and transforms the natural environment. By morally ordering the relations among those who fill its different economic and social statuses, such as managers and workers or buyers and sellers or parents and children and husbands and wives, it regulates the human species environment and thus provides the rights and privileges, the obligations and duties, for those who interact in a total social system.

These adaptive subsystems are in mutual dependence. The symbols of the moral order, those which convey the group's meanings for the rules governing human conduct and express its beliefs and values about right and wrong, good and bad, and what is to be rewarded or punished, are integral parts of the basic moral relation of the society with the animal life of the species.

Let us turn our attention to the other important concept mentioned in the question we asked earlier. What do we mean by emergent? The most general meaning, that of the dictionary, speaks of the appearance of new properties in the course of development and the origin of entirely new elements during the several phases of an entity's career. This, of course, includes all kinds of objects, both human and non-human. The term as here used is more limited and of greater scientific utility. It means, in brief, that the processes of change are in themselves integral parts of the social system, that the very nature of the system, if it persists in being what it is, must be in continual change—that each part has within it something coming into being and something ceasing to be. Moreover, it means that the cultural past is continually being absorbed into the present and the present into the future and that each loses part of its identity by this process of absorption. Our society cannot fulfill itself and be what it is at any moment in time unless it is always changing and becoming something else. Factually, this means that the younger generation, in school and elsewhere, learns new ways of thinking and doing, while the older generation must relearn and readjust to new ways in industry and government, and to new ways of organizing the public and private relations of everyone. It means that innovations themselves are constantly being reorganized and revaluated in terms of the old, that nothing is static, that all is movement and change. The significance of this social fact is also important for understanding the American individual, his personality and its development.

Change, being the nature of our social life, is consequently structured into the nature of each of us. What our society is now, what we are now and will be tomorrow, can be understood only in terms of the paradoxical fact that to be what we as individuals now are and for our society to be what it is, it and we must perforce be on the way toward being something different from what we are today. Consequently, all individuals in our culture, men and women, cannot stop

learning, on reaching maturity, as they do in most cultures. To maintain their adaptation to the real world around them—and in them,
for that matter—they must forever be learning to relate themselves
to a reality that is continually becoming something new. To be more
specific, our scientific technology and our highly rationalized society
(compared with the others) have research and change built into
them, and not only change but accumulated and accelerating change.
Moreover, while the common core values of our culture constantly
remold and tame the new developments in family life and in labor
and leisure as well as in politics and even in our conceptions of the
nature of the deity, emergent change is an integral part of them all.
New developments are not so much additions to the past as they
are emergent natural products of the immediate past.

We can go further and not only speak of the nature of emergent
change in America but identify some of its characteristics and point
out the directions in which this emergent system seems to be moving. Our society, as we said, demonstrates increasing heterogeneity.
It is moving constantly in that direction despite the influences of tradition, which tend to hold it toward a more homogeneous composition. With increasing heterogeneity there is an increasing need for
the coordination of the specialized and diverse parts. This necessarily
has an influence on the elaboration of coordinating statuses; the development of coordination with the need for decisions made by co-
ordinators usually places such statuses in superordinate, and those
coordinated in subordinate, positions. In brief, when these new positions are institutionalized, simple institutions expand into larger ones
and hierarchical systems develop where power and prestige are dif-
ferentially distributed according to the principles of hierarchy.

Our society moves in the direction of increasing control over the
physical and biological environments. This, in turn, places a greater
amount of power in the hands of people who operate its technological and moral adaptations. There is a relative and absolute increase
of the internal and external power used by those individuals who
make up our present population in our social system. This means
that there is an increase in the power exercised over the larger populations who make up the biological system and an increase of technological power over the natural environment. All of this increase in

power necessarily must be socialized and institutionalized. All of it has to have its technological form, and all of it must be ordered and regulated by our moral system. Sometimes, the accumulating increase of power comes with such accelerated activity that we find grave difficulty in knowing where to place it, what to do with it, and how to order it to transform it into our way of life. It takes more time to form what we must do into an ordered body of moral and mental propositions about how we must act as moral men.

Another characteristic of the direction of this emergent society is an increase in the velocity of change. Not only is change built into the system, but the rapidity of change is increasing. Moreover, as new change is structured into our world there seems to be an increasing capacity for more and more change to be absorbed into our social system.

Perhaps as another characteristic of our emergent world, the increasing velocity of change is closely related to the extension and improvement of the social techniques for introducing change into all living generations, not just in the younger ones. Individuals who, having learned earlier how to act adaptively, may not now know what is needed. The velocity of change is so great their own learning methods are not sufficient to permit them to make the adjustments necessary to act competently within new contexts. Adult and continuing education, night and correspondence schools, all of the other means that we have at the present time, such as in-plant training, are ways by which we more quickly incorporate new knowledge about our society into the lives of its individuals, making them more competent and reducing the number of possible casualties because of obsolescence.

Throughout all these developments, there have appeared new social usages and a reformation of older ones to contain and control the forces of diversity and expansion. Implied throughout this discussion is the concept of the moving social equilibrium, of adjustive change of the parts through time. There are certain basic adjustive processes operating in the moving equilibrium of this emergent society. At times it approximates a balance and at others an imbalance in the totality, or in some of the parts, as the society, so to speak, flows in the general direction of increasing diversity and greater differentiation through social, technical, and sacred experimentation. This tendency is always under the pressure of the conservative countertendencies of homogeneity. New developments may be merged into simpler forms of the old. There is a necessary reduction of variety. At the technological level new scientific knowledge and specialized skills and tools are invented, then rationalized and integrated into the basic and older forms of technological adaptation. Sometimes new inventions, as it were, sit hat in hand waiting their turn, redress themselves and change themselves, sometimes drastically, to fit the older ways of acting. At the level of the moral order new ways of acting and social subsystems come into being. Some of them are reworked into the older norms, each, the old and the new, being transformed in the process. The institution of the individual grocery store develops into a number of stores, and they in their turn become chain stores. Meanwhile, each becomes a supermarket, all of them with new ways of acting, new ways of marketing, new ways of relating the customer to the entrepreneur and the entrepreneur to the larger market where he buys his commodities. Yet a person returned from two generations back would recognize these present extraordinary institutions as stores and would soon know his way around them.

At the level of symbols and values, new and more specialized symbols and meanings appear. Some are translated into, or equated with, the older, more commonly understood forms and integrated into the common body of meanings. For example, some sects briefly come into being, find the going difficult and, as such, disappear. Others take on some of the old meanings of the society, to the point where they become growing sects and cults, which become denominations and highly respectable and integral parts of the larger moral and religious order. Christian Science, for example, had a rough, difficult beginning and is now, for most purposes, one of the several recognized ways by which Americans can relate themselves to God and to the world of the supernatural. Many of the Pentecostal cults, such as the Church of God, the Assembly of God, and others of their kind, were highly deviant and strange to conventional Americans; but they have now become stabilized denominations that play their accepted roles and relate themselves to the larger body of Protestantism in America.

Complex societies must have a common core of basic understanding known and used by everyone, or their complex and diverse symbolic superstructures will not stand. They need general symbol systems that everyone not only knows but *feels*. The increasing structural diversity and social complexity of contemporary society, the greater development of individual autonomy, the proliferation of specialized symbol systems—these and many other factors raise serious difficulties for communication and collaboration. If more and more problems are to be solved and greater and greater areas of reality comprehended and conquered, the social labor of a society must be increasingly divided and the advance in symbols must keep pace with technical and social achievement.

Experimentation, heterogeneity, specialization, increasing division of labor as well as velocity of change are partly restrained and contained by social forms and pressures which provide common experiences, common values, and common beliefs. The general tendency toward heterogeneity and diversity is counterbalanced by that toward homogeneity and uniformity; tendencies that make men and women different and difficult to approach in terms of their separateness from the commonalities are counterbalanced by those which lead them to the common places of cultural experience. Increased social mobility in America and the regional circulation of diverse people help reduce heterogeneity. Moreover, new laws, such as the taxation of income, social security, and many others, decrease social and economic difference and distance.

The increasing regional circulation with the need to fit not only one's immediate community and region but other regions too is beginning to be a part of the social structure of the total United States. Today a man who gets a job with Sears Roebuck in the South may in time learn how to adjust to a New England environment, and a New Englander to a southern one. All of this has drastic effects on the local cultures. This need to fit not only is a problem for the man who has a particular occupation in a specific business enterprise but also characterizes even more importantly the lives of his wife and children. They, too, move with him from place to place, learn how to change their thinking, and become changing people in a changing world.

The place of the local community is changing radically. It used to be the location where primary interaction took place, where face-to-face relations characterized the group life of men and women. At the present time, a larger community is coming into being, where direct action, communication, and face-to-face relations continue through the emergence of the great complex organizations in all parts of our lives, technological, moral, and sacred; largely because of this, men frequently interact with others over the whole United States.

In this world the great corporate hierarchies function, have their being, and are to be understood. In the next chapter we shall analyze the corporate hierarchy and its place in the great society. To do so it will be necessary to observe concomitant changes in big government and the peculiar functions of political parties in facilitating and curbing innovations and traditional ways of thinking and acting.

Big Corporations and

Big Government in the Great Society

INTRODUCTION: THE CORPORATION AS A SOCIAL SYSTEM

W<small>HAT</small> we look for in analyzing American society," Peter Drucker declares in *The Concept of a Corporation,* "is the institution which sets the standard for the way of life and the mode of living of our citizens which leads, molds, and directs; which determines our perspective on our own society; around which crystallize our social problems and to which we look for their solution. What is essential in society is, in other words, not the static mass but the dynamic element; not the multitude of facts but the symbol through which the facts are organized in a social pattern; not, in other words, the average but the representative. And this, in our society today, is the large corporation."

To the corporation must be added big government, particularly the new administrative and regulatory agencies, big unions, and in a special sense, the dual-party system. The last now functions with peculiar sensitivity and efficiency for the creation of the social system of the new society as the latter emerges from the multiplicity of smaller local communities. Secondarily, and at times primarily and dominantly, other great national institutions, including academic, ecclesiastical, and associational, also contribute importantly and uniquely to the emergent processes and to the structure and functioning of the contemporary American society.

The principal concern of this chapter is the great corporation and the great corporation as a moral and technical institution in the one community. But to understand it, other institutions and the way they operate must be examined. Given our problem and limited time, we shall necessarily be able to consider only some of them in order to concentrate on the corporation itself. However, attention must be given to big government and its agencies as part of the emergent national moral community that influences the corporation. The powerful and extraordinary effects of the dual-party system on the emergence of the new society, particularly on the evolvement of the regulatory and other central agencies of government as well as on the processes of social innovation and traditional behavior, must be explored. The dual-party system and the rising national public opinion and developing national moral order, the evolvement of big government and the emergence of the great corporation and the great society are all closely interrelated. Their relations and their significance for our problem will be outlined.

We will briefly inspect the rough object we shall later analyze and interpret. We shall first use the methods of common sense and the evidence ordinarily available about the American corporation. There are 4.5 million business enterprises in America, most of them very small and only 13 per cent corporations. Only a few of the latter are huge and dominant. Still, these large ones are of the greatest significance and importance for understanding American life. For example, of 263,000 firms in manufacturing, 361 corporations employ 40 per cent of all the employees in manufacturing. Similar figures might be cited for other types of business activity. All of this, of course, is well known and needs only to be brought to mind for our present purposes.

As a *legal* entity, the corporation is very old and has a long known history. Through time as a social and legal institution it has drastically changed. As early as the thirteenth century it was established in English law for ecclesiastical orders and for mercantile and craft guilds. By the fifteenth and sixteenth centuries it could sue and be sued and as a social entity it could and did persist beyond the lives of those who founded it. From the sixteenth to the nineteenth centuries it became a business organization, and from 1800 to 1890 it became easily available to all enterprisers and was routinely used by many to engage in business.

For understanding the corporation and the emergent society (but still as the rough object we shall later analyze), we must remember that in America the structure and technology of communication and transportation have played major roles in the development of the national society. Their national significance developed rapidly. For example, the first transcontinental railroad was built as late as 1869, but the first great railroad consolidations occurred from 1868 to 1880. In brief, at an early period in its own history the first major form of transportation became both technologically and institutionally national in its scope. The telephone patent came in 1876, but by 1900 the Bell Telephone Company, as a holding company, controlled a great national system of 1,350,000 telephones.

To speak at a somewhat more abstract and generalized level there has been a mounting concentration of corporate headquarters in a few communities. Two-thirds of the headquarters of the seven hundred largest corporations—banking, manufacturing, utilities, retailing, and transportation—are now located in the ten largest metropolitan centers. (This count excludes Washington, a political rather than an economic metropolis, where another large population manning another kind of great hierarchy is rapidly collecting.)

When viewed sociologically, the corporation and capitalistic enterprise in America form a vast, interconnected set of relations among the constituent parts, the whole composing an economic subsystem within the total society. The constituent parts are: (1) the structural form of economic life, which is an interrelated status system that orders the economic activities of those in the system; (2) the technology, which instrumentalizes the system and adapts the whole society to nature; and (3) the symbols, beliefs, and values of the system, including the conscious and unconscious feelings and rational principles which motivate and determine the behavior of those involved in the corporate and economic subsystem.

All of the parts are emergent and changing, each within itself, each with respect to the others, and each with respect to the total subsystem within the larger American society.

Through the increasing application of technical and scientific knowledge and the skillful use of tools and machines to provide for the material needs of the populace, this subsystem controls and transforms the natural environment. By morally ordering the relations among those who fill its different economic statuses, such as managers and workers or buyers and sellers, it provides the rights and privileges, the obligations and duties for those who work and for those who exchange goods and services in the American social system.

The whole economic system is animated by values, beliefs, and behavior which are expressed in the various relations and statuses composing the corporate structure and the entire system. The values and beliefs are the motivating forces and purposes which drive the economic agents of corporations to economic action. When expressed in action all such beliefs and values are reinforced by positive and negative sanctions: the former encourage men to do well and act according to the rules and values of the system; the latter discourage and help prevent behavior which violates the rules. Such sanctions curb and reduce varying kinds of aggressive and other antisocial acts not in conformance with the norms of the system. Negative sanctions can and do range from legal action—their sources in the laws of the country and its legal agencies—to vague, informal kinds of sanction, such as the satiric, where men are laughed at, scorned, or ridiculed by their fellows sufficiently to prevent them from continuing behavior that is believed reprehensible.

In this system the material and non-material objects of production, exchange, and distribution are both objects of utility and symbols of value. As such they belong to the symbolic and technical worlds of American life. They function as goals, ends, and sanctioning factors for those who participate in the system.

This economic subsystem and its several parts continually undergo change, the transition moving in a given direction toward increasing heterogeneity, diversity, acceleration of activity, and the increase of change itself. Although in theory, and, to a considerable degree, in fact, the classically ideal structure of American business enterprise is free, each economic institution of private enterprise conforms to, and is ordered by, the values and rules of the larger social system. Increasingly, corporate enterprise is dominated, bounded, and ordered by the federal, state, and municipal laws and by the pressures of great and little moral forces which are *not* economic.

In brief, emergent values, beliefs, moral controls, and many sanctions are increasingly influencing the actions and the developing structure of the corporation.

THE EMERGENT MORAL ORDER AND CORPORATE HIERARCHIES

Since 1900 this moral development has been a kind of dialectic and dialogue between the old and new values, beliefs, and moral opinions that are built into the processes of the American social system. From the end of the last century, and earlier for that matter, the national moral community and its law and sanctioning bodies began to emerge and increase their control. A combination of developing moral opinion, law, and national regulatory and administrative agencies has been operating. From 1865 to 1900, however, the values and beliefs of the theology of Calvin, the social Darwinism of Herbert Spencer, the earlier doctrine of the natural rights of man, and the rational doctrines of a free market combined to encourage the autonomous growth of the small and great corporations. These values, which defended the individual, were easily extended to include corporate freedom. The Supreme Court as a national entity was their principal agent. For example, the Fourteenth Amendment, placed in the Constitution to protect freed slaves, was used to rule against most efforts for legal control of corporations. From 1890 to 1910 under the due process clause of the Fourteenth Amendment there were only 19 decisions for freed slaves and 289 decisions for corporations. But at the turn of the century changing public moral opinion was given legal form in the Sherman Act (1890). A few years after, the name of Theodore Roosevelt, child labor laws, and the Pure Food and Drug Act appear, along with the name of Woodrow Wilson and anti-monopoly legislation shortly before the beginning of the First World War. From 1930 to now, as we all know, the rights of workers, the rise of unions, and other developments having to do with new conceptions about the collectivity, and the relations of the rational technology and the non-rational moral order continue the increasing legal and moral pressure on corporate freedom.

David E. Lilienthal, in his book *Big Business: A New Era,* declares: "Government has become an active and frequently the dominant factor in economic affairs. Today few important decisions are made by business executives and boards of directors in which some acts of government do not play a significant part. What is true of business also applies generally to farmers and workers in industry."

One of the classic historical periods of emergent change, in which moral power and its sanctions moved from local and private hands to those of the one great community, was the New Deal at the time of the Great Depression. Then and later the principles of economic rationality gave way to varying kinds of moral beliefs and values that were put into objective national law and made part of the formal system of American government. New administrative bureaus and regulatory agencies were created and, as integral parts of the structure of control, exercised enormous power over private enterprise.

The time when these new agencies appeared is significant in terms of the development of our understanding of the corporation and big business. Of the thirty independent administrative and regulatory agencies of greatest power and influence in Washington, only two were in existence by 1900 and five were created in the twenty years from 1900 to 1920. However, from 1920 to 1940, twelve of them were instituted. Of these, ten appeared in the period of the New Deal, from 1933 to 1940, that is to say, the period before the beginning of World War II when the domestic aspects of the New Deal were being pressed. From 1940 to 1960 eleven more of these large agencies were created. Four came into existence during a Republican administration including, perhaps significantly, the department called Health, Education and Welfare. The development of these great agencies, more often accelerated by the Democrats, is not entirely a Democratic and liberal process. We shall return to this matter later when we discuss political parties.

This great expansion of the federal and central structure is easily indicated by the growth of the number of employees in the Executive Branch of the government. In 1816 there were less than 5,000 men in the Executive Branch. By the time of the Civil War there were 36,000 in the entire Executive Branch and only 950 in the Department of Defense. By 1900 the numbers had risen to 230,000; twenty years later, to 650,000; and by 1940 for the first time the number of civilian employees rose to over 1,000,000 in the Executive Branch and over 250,000 in the Department of Defense. In 1959 there were 2,355,000 civilians employed by the Executive Branch of the federal government.

A recent (Republican and Democratic) example of the developing structure of moral opinion at the national level, not quite so prominent but far reaching in its effect, is the Committee on Government Contracts. The government as a client and contractor for a substantial part of the business now taking place in the United States is in a strong position to exercise moral power over private economic practices. A small, powerful committee under the control of the Vice President puts pressure on private enterprise throughout the United States to expand opportunities for minority groups, particularly Negroes and Jews. The membership of the committee is so constituted that, in fact, it acts as a moral pressure group at the highest executive level; the influence of the Presidency is often felt immediately by recalcitrant small and large economic enterprises; none of this behavior has to do with free economic enterprise; rather, all of it is the moral order acting through law on corporate hierarchies. Sanctions are brought to bear on profit-making organizations to force them to obey the moral rules and basic values of a democratic society.

Although the entrepreneur, held within the limits of new and traditional law and established practice, is no longer a free agent, he still is free to strive to increase his profit. The deep motivations of profit-making still exist. They are of paramount importance for understanding why men in private enterprise act as they do and for knowing why they spend their lives and devote their energies to careers which entirely absorb most of them. However, if the entrepreneur succeeds in making a profit, an increasing share is taken from him. The income, excess profit, and many other taxes now take a large part of what the enterpriser makes, to be used for the collectivity and to make it possible for his powerful rival, the huge hierarchical government structure, to be financed.

As a matter of fact, the larger the income the higher the proportion of the profits of the enterpriser taken by the government. This is not freedom of action nor does it conform to the old rule that the entrepreneur should be allowed, and be rewarded by, the greatest profit he is capable of making in the free market. The standards and values of the society have changed, and so have the values and behavior of the enterpriser.

If his own (and his corporation's) standards of conduct are not sufficient to cause obedience to the developing rules and values now emerging, then a decent respect for the opinions of his peers and fellow citizens may prompt him; often, when even this fails, prudence and common sense enlighten his self-interest and force conformance. It may not be economically sensible but it is morally wise. If such wisdom fails to function, then legal sanctions of the central government may be expected.

In the light of what Adolph Berle wrote in 1933 about private property and the corporation before the rapid advance by the new agencies in Washington it is instructive to note that in his introduction to *The Corporation in Modern Society,* published last year, he said the corporation's "role was not purely economic, though to be so was indeed its primary function, nor purely commercial, though profit was surely its purpose. It subtly changed both practice and theory of private property. It shifted substantial areas of production and exchange from a free market to an administered price system. It developed a vast, non-Statist organization of men and finance, an organization which increasingly raises problems of power. More recently we are beginning to see a pattern for distribution of its profits, suggesting an eventual non-Statist socialization of these profits, unique in its institutional impact. Slowly—or perhaps not so slowly —industrial United States is moving toward a form of economic republic without historical precedent."

In his book *The Twentieth Century Capitalist Revolution* (1954) Berle examines a number of allied problems about the corporation and its place in contemporary society. He is interested in the limitations that surround its economic power, not so much those of the market place, but the kinds of social and legal pressures that bind those who direct great corporations. The principal limitations on the corporation at the present time, he believes, are moral and practical: its men want to stay in business; its managers and owners want to be able to lead them. They realize that if they misbehave not only may they lose control of the corporations, but the corporation itself may disappear, becoming an adjunct of the state. The corporation responds to the power of public opinion, to the beliefs and values that have been rapidly developing which lead them from the robber baron period over to economic and social responsibility.

THE EMERGENT PROCESS AND THE DUAL-PARTY SYSTEM

Although we have spoken of the influences of homogeneity and tradition we have largely given our attention to the innovating and heterogeneous aspects of the emergent process and to movements away from the past. This has been particularly true of the national government and the creation of agencies for moral change at the national level. Examining new law, new agencies, and recent Supreme Court decisions tells much, but not all, of the story. The functioning of political parties to maintain a continuing equilibrium between the movements of variety and change and those of homogeneity and tradition must be analyzed.

Our thesis about the dual-party system is simple. As the great corporations, big unions, and other complex organizations expand and take on new meanings and functions, the moral behavior and values of public opinion grow and expand. Laws are passed, Supreme Court decisions made, new agencies created to contain and control these developments. The political parties have been the principal instruments to facilitate collective action at the national level, but the dual-party system is so related to developing public and moral opinion that the total effect is to reduce much of the potential heterogeneity and innovation that might come into being were the two parties differently related to public opinion and to the structure of the federal system. The dual-party system acts as a stabilizing mechanism between the new and the old to maintain equilibrium among the parts of the great community. It is true that many new laws and many new regulatory agencies operate today to expand the moral opinion of the great society, but our dual-party system primarily operates to maintain social cohesion. As such, the capitalistic system and the corporate structure are freer and less controlled than would be true were our party system to function as parties do in many western European countries.

Our political parties are action groups which, in varying degrees, express the multiple beliefs and values that are consequences of the heterogeneity of status and the rapid social change which are integral parts of this emergent society. The processes of social renewal, ever a part of this kind of changing society, transform and re-express the values of the past as they reincorporate the traditional social forms into contemporary ones. New political and social values, new activities and beliefs, are implicated with and re-formed into the solid social forms of the past. The dual-party system takes on this logically contradictory but socially congruent task, symbolically expressing new values and beliefs and in fact putting them into action. The expanding heterogeneous social structure, with its increasingly diverse activities, for purposes of equilibrium necessarily feels the pull of the central normative rules and values, which restrain and constrain. The two parties function to reduce the rapidity of change; they help pull back new diversities into old uniformities. The heterogeneous extremes are often tested by them and either excluded, dropped, or incorporated into customary forms. Often, the best ideas of third parties are necessarily stolen, thus maintaining the dual-party order and allowing it to continue functioning in its present capacity. The two parties may help adapt new ideas in such a way that older social forms undergo transformation, some being dropped or re-formed into new meanings and activities.

The stabilizing institutions, such as the family, school, and church, the conservative values of prestige classes, the close integration through social mobility of social classes, the centrifugal pull of diverse economic classes, usually with common tasks necessary for individual and group survival, the inertia of the very old and the conservatism of the very young, and many other factors, also help pull back the widely expanded and often overextended complex American group to a position nearer what we may call the center. The political party structure, strongly influenced by the slow-moving governmental one, helps maintain the solid core of custom and conformity while incorporating new developments of the society into acceptable usages of the changing social structure.

Apart from outside pressure, which we disregard for the time being, rapid social changes that need political sanction for their establishment usually occur when disfunctional processes have appeared in the society or its economy. When the political center is strong, both at the level of the voter and in the legislative and executive departments, it is likely that the social changes taking place do so with a high degree of social equilibrium. When the center is weak, conflict is far more likely, and disequilibrium between the parts is present. A strong center is likely to reduce the anxieties and hostilities felt by those at either end of the political range, particularly when their feelings are products of the transitions of this society. The extremes, conservative or liberal, as the case may be, feel encouraged or discouraged as more of the past is held to, and incorporated into the present, or as more of the innovations now associated with the possible future and with progress are introduced as political and social reforms.

In this society the center functions to reduce some of the frustration and anxiety of the two extremes and helps maintain equilibrium. In times of social tranquillity or under great external stress, little of the possible future is likely to be introduced into our political life. In times of internal crisis and sometimes during war the center may function in such a way as to collaborate with the liberal extreme and rapidly sanction new developments.

In speaking of the center as a necessary and significant part of our dual-party system, one would suppose that there were at least three principal parties. Everyone knows that this is not the case. In America, liberal and conservative opinions are distributed through both parties, sufficiently unequally, however, so that one party has more of the conservatives and less of the liberals, whereas the other has many more liberals than conservatives. We thus have the two parties related to the government structure in such a way that the party in power brings with it political beliefs and values which may range throughout the normal political spectrum. Meanwhile, the opposition is composed of members with similar differences of opinion.

Power and opinion are thus spread throughout the range of those who control the government, but the opposition presently finds out (in varying degrees) that at least some of what it believes and holds to is being put into action by those who now exercise the controls.

If my analysis is correct, the unity of American society and the stabilization of corporate structures are probably increased by the distribution of some of the same diverse and conflicting political beliefs and values in each party. As a result, to maintain party cohesion, it is necessary to exert strong influences through the propagation of the values of party loyalty and through the pressure of the internal organization of each party on its members, so that through the processes of compromise the extremes are pulled together. Meanwhile, moiety rivalry and competition allow many hostilities within the party to be expressed in an orderly and acceptable form against the opposing group. Factional hostilities within each party, often more powerful than between them, are thus brought under manageable control, and the felt need for aggressive action is expressed outside each political group. This action is facilitated by the desire to win the election, to defeat the enemy, and to take the strongholds of government power from the opposition. Individuals here are not necessarily committed to either party. They can and do change sides. Part of the time, social changes are accomplished or prevented by the movement of the independent and uncommitted voters and their representatives across party lines.

In terms of the political sentiments and values of this changing society, the members of the political parties move forward or back, and must do so if (at times of election) they are to maintain party loyalty and organizational unity while trying to capture the independent voters and some of the members of the other party. Partly because the diverse groups in the electorate and among their political representatives fear to isolate themselves too completely, the center in both parties ordinarily stays large and strong. Large numbers of representatives thus tend to edge toward the center because it represents safety, compromise, uniformity, and the likelihood of a majority vote. The center also stays large in part because most voters occupy the many social, ethnic, and economic statuses in the middle of the social structure, where the feelings, beliefs, and values are within the central norms of the group. Moderation fits their own needs and their view of the immediate and distant worlds around them. To win national elections, all significant varieties of opinion must be appealed to. At such times the center must and can extend itself, or appear to yield to both the conservative and the liberal extremes. At other times the right and the left more often yield to the center.

The consequences of these several factors—the spread of diverse opinion in each party, the spirit and conscious need of compromise, the functioning of a strong center, and the values and pressures of party loyalty combined with the threatened or actual movement of votes from party to party—have resulted in strengthening the unity of the country at the political level and discouraging drastic changes that might have resulted in sectional, class, or other forms of social conflict. Should the distribution of liberal and conservative opinions be polarized at their extremes and should the moderate center disappear and the two parties express opinions and hostilities of the extreme right and left, then many of the latent conflicts in our social structure would be likely to become open and dangerous, resulting in violence, disorder, and consequent tyranny, with the possible development of a coercive police state and other revolutionary activity.

In this matrix of two parties and the spread of liberal and conservative opinion in both, the more traditional opinions about property, corporate structure, and free enterprise maintain their being while big government grows and its agencies expand and increase their significance to confront the increasing strength of the great corporations. The functioning of the two-party system allows both governmental and economic advance, yet reduces the amount and kind of each. The dual-party system with diverse opinion in both parties is of vital importance in maintaining the kind of changing society America now is. Let us once again turn our attention to the corporation.

THE CORPORATION AND THE NEW SOCIETY

Clearly, the positive rights of natural man, embodied in the values and beliefs of those who founded our charters of collective life, those that lie implicitly within classical economics and politics, are now less valued than formerly. Since the middle of the last century and the beginning of this one, the underlying moral order, in which these beliefs and values about our corporate life must operate, has changed sufficiently so that the older beliefs are now given less and less attention, have less strength, or have taken on new meanings in the mental life of Americans. The crucial test of all this is that the entrepreneur (or the corporation) cannot charge what the market place will permit nor can he keep what the profit motive has led him to acquire.

Federal regulation of buying and selling, the regulation of the money supply, of minimum wages and maximum hours, and many other activities new to the province of the great government hierarchies are formal legal expressions of the basic processes of change in the moral values that increasingly control this technical and economic life of the larger society. In this sense, and paradoxically, although the society increasingly is using a non-moral technology and the cold rationality of science, American capitalistic enterprise is less and less dominated by the rational values of the technology (and those of classical economics); increasingly, it feels and yields to the influence of the non-rational value system of the moral order.

Sanctions now are both technical and moral, whereas at one time they were ideally technical, and a man succeeded or failed according to the intelligent decisions he made in the market place. At present he may make "intelligent" decisions and very well fail. Often it will be because of the many changes that have occurred in the informal moral structure and value system of this society. Now his advantages and choices are limited. He cannot operate the kind of enterprise that privately he might wish to—one that formerly would have been profitable and acceptable.

The interplay of the opposing forces of the non-rational moral structure and the rationality of the expanding technology is a basic theme that we must explore with great care because it is the area where we will learn perhaps the most about the development of these two fundamental hierarchies, the corporate and the political; more importantly, it is where we will learn the kinds of new values emerging and coming into being for the moral control of the increasing rationality of our mental life and the pragmatic behavior of the members of the emergent community.

Still, the structure of economic enterprise remains private and competitive; those who manage and lead are out to make a profit. Despite management's continuing desire for profit, modern labor, although "salable goods" and a commodity in the market place, now has its recognized moral claim to a just share of the profits. For some workers this can be taken by an annual wage, but more often these beliefs and values about the workers' advancing rights and status lie implicitly within the thinking of Americans. There is now a firm moral resolve that never again can there be a depression, where destitute people starve in bread lines simply because of the "natural" force of a non-moral economic law. Once again rationality, so-called, yields to the deep, non-rational forces of the moral order. Covariantly in the emergent process, the status of the worker is increasingly defined in moral rather than technical terms and those of impersonal rationality; increasingly, the status of worker is a position of several dimensions, not one; meanwhile, the capitalist's status and the manager's, in this same process are being redefined and revaluated more in conformance with the written and oral law of the moral order.

Capitalistic enterprise, still founded on exchange, through the instrument of contract viably and powerfully continues in the market place. But the market is no longer only for economic agents; its stage is now crowded with many actors. Prices now are partly a product of the direct intervention of government, or the pressure of unions on government, or the practical ethics of trade associations on their own members. The market place, where formerly the higglings of buyers and sellers made up the entire decisive and legitimate actions which produced Adam Smith's prices, now yield some of their power to moral agents. The recent Congressional hearings on the prices of drugs and their relations to such professions as pharmacology and medicine are producing a strong moral reaction. The manufacturers were out to sell their goods for the highest profit the market would bear, a principle that once was considered noble, worthy, and the only one that should be allowed to operate in a free society. It aligned human fallibility to the high-minded, rational, economic principles of a mental checkerboard. Now, following such principles, drug entrepreneurs feel the reprobation of most Americans and fear legal developments. All that the market will bear is no longer all that the emergent moral values of public opinion will bear. Government investigation informs public opinion and then acts as its moral agent. Although law increases its own importance in capitalistic enterprise, what is involved in the contractual arrangements increasingly includes what an older generation of anthropologists called status. Beyond contract, the society recognizes the larger moral being in the capitalistic roles of its members.

Some of the knowledge about the principal values, beliefs, and behavior of contemporary American capitalism can be formally stated in testable propositions:

Acquisition and profit are the ends of enterprise, but these must be necessarily modified and controlled by, and for, the larger collectivity. Profit-making in itself is good, but it is not good enough.

Competition in itself is an end as well as a means, but it, too, necessarily must be regulated, morally controlled from without, and modified by cooperation from within an industry or confederation of allied industries. Trade associations are increasingly numerous and powerful among the varying kinds of enterprise in America. Professional associations, composed of tens of thousands of members from the physical, biological, and human sciences, who use their knowledge and skills for corporate competitive gain, cause the powerful moral pressures of long-established ethical codes to be newly applied to the new definitions of market behavior.

The relative values of the individual enterpriser and the corporate individual in competition with others are better than the absolutes of monopoly. The uncontrolled exercise of monopolistic power, of total success in defeating competitors, now is not a "natural" right in the American mores. Nor can the enterpriser and his managers extend their control as far as their power will go. As far as their power will go here means as far as their economic power would permit them in competition with others. The du Ponts, for example, in some of their enterprises could easily wipe out their competitors. However, should they do so they would immediately find themselves in many difficulties that would open their private defenses and make them vulnerable to public reprisals that would threaten their autonomy. At the least, such difficulties could be far more irritating and much more expensive to them than if they restrain themselves. This restraint on free market power is felt so strongly by the du Ponts and others that they allow their competitors to use some of their own marketable goods and patented processes to help them do a better job competing against them. For example, du Pont fabrics patents are now leased to some of their competitors. The du Ponts, of course, are well aware of what they are doing. They feel they must control themselves if they are not to be controlled completely by others. The meanings that cluster around unrestrained monopoly in this society have very strong negative undertones which arouse deep hostility, particularly when a monopoly controls a commodity that could be competitive in the market place. The du Ponts do not choose to be put on the defensive in this unpleasant position.

Despite the many changes emerging in private enterprise, which control its competitive freedom, the basic proposition—that the risk-taker must gain or suffer the consequences of his actions—animates much of the behavior in the market place. It is based on the fundamental belief that the autonomous person and his corporate entity must gain or suffer by the choices they make.

The increase in specialization and the division of job statuses into smaller and less skilled units is one of the noticeable processes taking place in contemporary American industrial society. These increasingly are interrelated by mechanical, highly rationalized, and simplified methods, so that the job flow, in producing a product, is in fact (or has a quality of being) an assembly line, some of it subject to, or having passed into, automation. (We are in no way attempting to say that some of the developments which we have mentioned and which are parts of the changing structure of American social life are not present elsewhere. What we are saying is that they are here and that when seen in their entirety they make up a system that has its own unique variety of being.)

Mechanical specialization and the differentiation of job status are an interdependent, interconnected process. The influence is not one way, from the technology to status differentiation of the jobs, nor is it necessarily from the social structure and the mental life of the people to the technological system of any particular enterprise; the three—moral, mental, and technical—are parts of the process of emergence.

The tendencies toward specialized technical skills and simplified job statuses under many circumstances have meant more jobs and the probability of a larger population involved in any given corporate enterprise. This has increased the problem of relating the workers to each other and to those who supervise them. Within the limits of these corporate structures the whole problem of coordination becomes of very great importance, often resulting in an hierarchical arrangement. Too many hierarchies and too many levels in a hierarchy create inefficiency and can result in modified chaos. On the other hand, too many people at one level without proper coordination and without some kind of hierarchical order also make it impossible for the varying specialized groups to collaborate efficiently in getting the work done. Consequently, in separate private corporations the vertical and horizontal status structures are greatly increased not only in a given enterprise but throughout the total economy.

The accelerating process of reclassification of jobs and statuses, which lumps varieties of workers together, this associated with increasing similarity among jobs, with the loss of worker skill, and the increase of mechanization, may be a transitory form whose ultimate result may be the automation of all technological activities. If that process continues, automation will invade some of the higher levels of middle management and, in time, take over some of the prerogatives of management. The meanings of this ultimate seizure of moral power for our social order are not known. They must be examined and studied.

The increasing heterogeneity has been accompanied by the incorporation of smaller units of enterprise into large-scale complex organizations. These combinations, in their time, increase supervisory tasks and often result in the proliferation of staff and supervisory statuses. Corporations with many satellite organizations are integral parts of this kind of process. Some of the vast cartels, interrelated by common managements and common boards, are also extreme varieties of this same process. All instances of the increasing proliferation of great hierarchies introduce problems about placement of power and concern about the maintenance of control, cohesion, and proper communication among the levels of people charged with the operation of these great organizations.

The technology of American capitalism, as we said earlier, is characterized by the application of rational principles, knowledge, and skills of science. Since science is founded on the principle of increasing the body of valid knowledge about man and nature, the amount and variety of scientific knowledge applied to the control of nature increase economic control over it and, indirectly, social control. Scientific inventions and patents are used for competitive advantage. In many industries, planned, researched inventions, protected by patents, outstrip all other competitive efforts to increase profit and gain. The investment of money, time, and brains in science makes up a larger and larger proportion of the budget of many of the great industrial organizations. Many put their money in various laboratories or in the research enterprises of great universities; others maintain great research institutions and research organizations of their own.

From 1850 to 1900 there were tens of thousands of independent inventors. Their inventions were patented and greatly contributed to the expanding American technology. The first American research laboratory started by private industry was not established until 1900, but by the beginning of World War I there were a hundred corporations with research departments, and these grew to some three hundred by the end of that war. Since 1925 the number of independent inventors has decreased greatly. Meanwhile, there has been a growth of scientific technology, rationality, and planning, and of employment of engineers, chemists, and scientists by corporate research, combined with the growth of large-scale corporations and the control of patents and inventions by these private enterprises. (This does not mean to say that small corporations are not contributing at least, or perhaps more than, their proportionate share to invention and technological advancement.)

The National Science Foundation recently reported that 15,500 firms now have research and development staffs. However, 44 large firms employ 45 per cent of the scientists and spend 50 per cent of the money. Some 435 million dollars are spent in America on basic research. Corporations spend 40 per cent of it and do 40 per cent of the work; universities and other non-profit organizations spend 25 per cent and do 50 per cent of the work; while government spends 35 per cent and does 10 per cent of the work.

During the last century, science was largely used in the capitalistic economy to break through the resistances of nature. In the first half of this century, capitalism has greatly expanded its use of the social and psychological sciences to understand human beings. For management of corporations and other large-scale hierarchies, with these rationalistic processes in being, it is only a matter of time until mechanical operations will reduce and treat much of the pleasant but irritating individual variability now thought of as *personality* differences to the flat, technical sortings of IBM cards. The invasion of the non-rational moral order by the rationality of the scientific technology continues; yet (as we said earlier) as these developments emerge, the counterforces of the moral order of the national community assert themselves.

The incorporation of smaller units into larger ones, marked in most enterprises, reduces local-community autonomy and increases the strength of national enterprises with common centers of control. The lateral extension of vast enterprises throughout the country, associated with the elaboration of corporate and other hierarchies to manage such enterprises, increases, as we said, the circulation of the managerial elite from community to community and reduces the proportion of those of high status who live out their lives in one place. Simplification of skill and jobs, improved transportation and communication, have partly freed the workers, too, and increased the number of them who move from place to place. These workers are less dependent on their employers in one locality and on one kind of job in one industry. The result is greater fluidity in the labor market and, more importantly, a freer status for the worker. Once he had to learn and embody his skills. While this gave him a certain advantage in getting jobs, it bound him to the few skills which fitted a particular job and a particular kind of industry. With the breakdown of skill hierarchies into simplified positions and with the mechanization of many of these positions, many workers can be quickly trained, so that they can take new jobs that fit many of the mechanized categories of the new technology.

This process makes it possible, other restraints not interfering, for them to move not only from one particular corporation to another within a given industry, but from industry to industry. This facilitated circulation of the working classes through various occupations allows them to move with easy competence from place to place and from job to job. Today, economic and skill restrictions are not what prevent men from moving; social constraints and benefits (such as concern about keeping their children in school and in one place, seniority, security, or clinging to a style of life) may keep them where they are; even so, choices to stay or go are now technologically possible.

All of these developments are parts of the elaboration of the great society territorially. Primary face-to-face interaction, once largely characteristic of the local community, is increasingly extended to the one great community—from San Francisco to New York; from Bangor, Maine, to San Diego, California; from the smallest village in Alabama to the smallest community high in the Rockies of Idaho. The increasing circulation and daily interaction of the elite of business and governmental enterprises are parts of a spatial and time movement of many kinds of people.

These changes are facts and symbols of the transition of our people at all levels as integral elements in the multiple process by which corporate and other complex structures expand as the local collectivities increasingly lose their autonomy to the moral authority of the new national community that is now in being.

Autonomous Man

and the Corporate Process

IN earlier pages, the social and economic worlds of the modern corporation have been discussed, with emphasis on the group rather than the individual, on the nature of emergent change as a *social* rather than an *individual* process.

In this part we turn our attention to individuals, to those who are members and leaders of giant corporations; they will be the objects of interest and the units of analysis. We shall first learn what they are as persons, then empirically determine the mental and moral demands of high managerial positions, the tough and real criteria for successful performance. Thus, we shall discover what kinds of persons executives are, what it takes to be one, and see how they fit the top positions. We can then relate the persons themselves and their corporate positions to the meanings of the emergent processes of the great society, the one primary community. All of the generalizations come from long-time field researches on personality in the great corporate, government, and other large-scale organizations in this society.

Before continuing we must take a brief moment to comment on the most often quoted and best known book on today's executives, William H. Whyte's *The Organization Man*. His book is an attack on what the author conceives to be the supine yielding of corporate men to collective pressures. They do not make their individual decisions, according to Mr. Whyte, from within themselves as autonomous men; their decisions come from the corporate collectivity outside them. "Organization men" are not individuals; they are not autonomous but automata. Mr. Whyte declares that his book is "about the organization man— The corporation man is the most conspicuous example,

47

but he is only one, for the collectivization so visible in the corporation has affected almost every field of work." These men are dominated by what he says he is going to call—"a Social Ethic." With reason it could be called an organization ethic—that contemporary body of thought which makes morally legitimate the pressures of society against the individual. Its major propositions are three: a belief in the group as a source of creativity; a belief in "belongingness" as the ultimate need of the individual; and a belief in the application of science to achieve the belongingness.

Mr. Whyte attacks this whole position largely, it seems, for fallacious reasons. But his own words make far more sense than the popular application of them in pulpit, court, and press. The organization man, to many, means a person who is a puppet, one whose movements are controlled by others and who, as a puppet, is incapable of initiating movement and making his own decisions. Mr. Whyte, of course, is not entirely to blame for his popular following; still he has provided a fallacious theme which makes it easy for others to develop their own fallacies.

The picture of the executive that I will present is the exact opposite of Whyte's caricatures. Evidence will be supplied from extensive research by myself and others to argue that big business leaders as persons are autonomous and that they usually make their own decisions. It will be demonstrated that to be successful and to meet the demands of the high positions they occupy they must be capable of autonomous decision-making.

It is time to define more precisely what is meant by autonomy. Autonomy does not necessarily mean behavior that is contrary to the basic rules and demands of social organization. It is here that Mr. Whyte and others assume an opposition that is not necessarily present. Essentially, by an autonomous person I refer to that man or woman who has internalized his experiences in the society in such a way that he is able to make his own decisions *from within,* rather than being completely dependent upon the influences and instructions coming from without. This means that he is morally autonomous, in the sense that he can apply the rules of the society himself, by his own decisions, that he knows and can act on what is right and wrong, and intellectually he is capable of making the discriminations that are necessary in a fluid society to operate in positions that are often ambiguous. (Essentially, this definition comes from the conceptions and research of Jean Piaget, who very early contributed to our understanding of the mental and moral development of individuals in modern society.) Given this definition, it can now be said that being morally autonomous does not mean that the individual is completely different or stands completely on his own. He necessarily has internalized the social world around him and its mental and moral rules sufficiently so that he himself can, with due regard to the realities of the outside world, apply his decisions, his judgments, and his mental concepts to himself and others; he makes his own decisions but does so as a member of his culture and his group.

We can now turn our attention directly to the evidence about the personalities of the individual business leaders. We can ask ourselves: What are the personality characteristics of big business leaders? What kinds of personalities do the individual executives tend to have? Are they organization men without the moral and mental capacity for individual decision, bowing almost unknowingly and automatically to the outward authority of others? Or are they autonomous, capable of playing the game according to the rules, and able to make their own decisions from within themselves? (This, of course, does not necessarily mean that some of these men may not at times act unethically and break some of the basic rules of the game itself.) Our evidence comes from a study, by Dr. James Abegglen and myself, of some eight thousand executives of big business, representing all types of industry. A small sample of the eight thousand men was restudied by psychological and depth analysis. Both depth interviews and Thematic Apperception Tests were used. The statements made here are also founded on the work of Professor William E. Henry, of the University of Chicago, on successful and unsuccessful businessmen and on evidence from an approximately fifteen-year study of several thousand executives by Social Research Incorporated of Chicago. The latter sample and Professor Henry's include all levels and all kinds of executives, both successes and failures.

All of the corporate executives in the Warner-Abegglen study had personalities with high mobility drives. There is in all of these successful men a deep and constant motivation for upward mobility, for striving with a kind of primitive feeling for upward movement. Closely associated with this feeling is an ever greater need for the increased responsibility that comes with advancement. Such men obtain a deep feeling of satisfaction that is directly related to finishing one task in order to start the next one. Such individuals look upon themselves as hard-working men who cannot be happy unless achieving and accomplishing the work tasks that need to be performed. According to Professor Henry, the successful executive "looks more to the sheer accomplishment of the work itself" than to the secondary glory that may be attached to what it is that has been performed. This is in strong contrast to the kind of man who is upward-mobile and strives to advance himself but who is more interested in the struggle for social prestige; his immediate thoughts are around status advancement rather than work achievement and the rewards that come directly from it. The first kind of man tends to be more successful and get to high position. The second is likely to find moving up the corporate ladder more difficult.

Perhaps one of the most significant personality characteristics of the successful corporation executive is his conception of authority; this is of crucial importance to interpret properly the actions of an executive at a top-level position. Such a man looks to his superiors for guidance and help and feels happier when he is directly involved with them in what often is a controlling relationship. He can believe, and does, that a good superior is someone to whom he can go for consultation, for advice of higher quality, and for special help when it is needed. Above all, he does not see figures of authority as destructive and likely to be damaging and thwarting to his own career. He may see them and their positions, because of the realities about him, as temporarily preventing advancement. But this is not so much attributed to the personal characteristics of the men above him as to the corporate situation which confronts anyone dealing with the realities of life.

All such upward-mobile men who are successful in their business enterprises have a high ability to organize situations and to understand the meaning and significance of what it is that they have organized. They do not see events as isolated and unconnected but as interrelated, and they draw significance from the interrelationships.

In other words, they are constantly making decisions and judgments based on their organizing ability in a social structure which is ever changing, where new adaptations are forever necessary for the success of the person and the success of the enterprise. They have personalities capable of holding together the parts of a changing society.

Successful executives have the great ability to make the necessary mental judgments and arrive at the necessary moral conclusions in a great variety of ambiguous situations which disturb and distress all men at high position and to make their decisions in such a way that appropriate action can be taken. In brief, the flow of events related to the changing structure of corporate enterprise and to the rapidly changing technology are presented to, and managed by, them in such a way that their decisions contribute to the direction of successful corporate action. Those who do not succeed in doing this fail to rise to or maintain position at the top levels of the business hierarchy. From the studies of unsuccessful businessmen, who have not risen or who have had grave difficulties, it becomes evident that their decisions are frequently suffused with anxiety. They find great trouble in easily making the decisions necessary for the continuing advance of the corporation. For them the great variety of alternatives, the ambiguities of the immediate present as they are related to the more distant future, are much too troublesome and frustrating.

The most important component of the personalities of successful corporate managers and owners is that, their deep emotional identifications with their families of birth being dissolved, they no longer are closely intermeshed with the past and, therefore, are capable of relating themselves easily to the present and future. They are people who have literally and spiritually left home. However, the separation from the past, particularly from the deep emotional identification with early family relations, does not involve hostility or apathy. Easy relations with the parents usually exist. In brief, these men are so constituted personally that they can relate to the immediate present without the past controlling their decisions. They can think about and act in the flow of the future as they move with it. They can relate and disrelate themselves to others easily. The basic and fundamental problem of successfully "leaving home" that faces all men has been solved, and thus they have early set the pattern of relations with those around them as they move into maturity. They are able to break close ties with others; but they have the emotional capacity, as many able men do not, of maintaining feelings of warmth and closeness while keeping sufficiently detached so that, in the developing sequence of their careers, they can continue to relate themselves to other corporate men. They accomplish the basic tasks of mobility for themselves and adjust the present of the corporation to its future needs. Moreover, as mobile men and as men who relate their present to the immediate and more distant future, they have the capacity to scrutinize the present to learn how to move ahead in their own lives and in the life of the corporation. Consciously or unconsciously, they have faith in the flexibility of the world around them, in its fluidity, so that as leaders they can contribute to the direction of the outcomes of any given sequence of events for themselves and the institution which they lead.

Psychic analysis of the personalities of these men shows that on the whole their energies, their sense of the moral rules, the Protestant design of their ethical behavior (whether they be Protestants or not), and their social goals seem to derive largely from their experiences with their mothers. The father in fantasy is usually the more unreliable figure. Often there is a feeling of deprivation and a sense of loss with the image of the father, a feeling that the father is withholding something that can only be gained from other father figures in the world around them. All of this, of course, derives from the early formative stages of the personality and carries on through life.

In summary, the personalities of corporate executives, those who reach the top or who are on their way toward the top, are not lacking in self-reliant abilities; they stand on their own, as self-contained, autonomous members of the team. Morally, they have internalized the rules of the social world around them and are capable of directing themselves and others in a rapidly changing world. Intellectually, they examine the changing world and make decisions that, many times and in many places, are demanded in a fluid, unstructured society. Their personality characteristics identify them not as supine "organization" robots, but as autonomous individuals who have succeeded and who have maintained autonomous personalities. (It must be remembered that this is a report on the central tendencies of such men; here we cannot give all variations.)

THE DEMANDS OF CORPORATE LEVELS ON EXECUTIVE DECISIONS

The executives studied were on the average between fifty-four and fifty-five years old. Through their lives most had climbed from lower to higher positions in the greatest corporations in America. The problem that now arises is: Why were men with autonomous personalities more often found at these higher levels of business and the great corporations than other types of personality. One must ask: What is demanded of them mentally and emotionally, as they move from level to level, from lower to higher jobs? What kinds of decisions are required by the different corporate statuses of a man as he moves to the top?

For a considerable period of time the social and psychological sciences have been greatly interested in the nature of decision-making, particularly in business enterprise. For over a decade the nature of decision-making and its meanings and significance for the corporate structure, have been under careful study in one of America's very largest corporations. The principal research in this particular effort has been done by Professor Norman Martin, of New York University. From his results we can learn how the sifting process operates at the different levels of corporate management. Let us first define what is meant by decision-making in business. We will follow Professor Martin, who declares: "A managerial decision is a present commitment to a particular line of action based upon anticipation of the future course of events."

All decisions of managers take place in an existing situation— what we shall call, with Professor Martin, the decision-making situation. To understand and explain the decision-making process of all managers and the differences among decisions in the corporate hierarchy, we must place each decision in its immediate job context within the hierarchy, within the complex of relations that make up the corporate structure. We must say, too, what takes place in the several aspects of time which make up the decision itself. With these two principles to guide us, the first about place in the hierarchical structure itself and the second about time, we can now ask research-able questions and gain first answers with moderately exact measurements for evidence.

The questions we must ask are: Do the decisions at the different levels of management, top, bottom, and intermediate, differ, or are they similar? Are the durations of time the same at the higher and lower levels? Finally, are the several levels of management the same or different for the elements of continuity and the duration of effective action?

By duration we refer to the relative extension into the past and future of a sequence of events having to do with a decision. It may be far in the past or future or confined to the near present. Time perspective defines the event. By continuity we mean that the temporal series of acts may be continuous or discontinuous. There may be a continuous flow of action, or there may be few or many intervals. (The interval defining the break, in the research situation which we are reporting, was one working day.) To manage the study and make it possible to report on the events observed, the research divided the duration of a decision into three lengths, referred to by the common-sense terms, short, moderate, and long. The short events were divided into two—those lasting less than a week and those from one to two weeks. Moderate duration was from two weeks to a month and from one month up to a year. In the last major category were all decisions comprising any sequence of events that lasted over a year.

The various positions of management were divided into four levels. They were the highest level of top management, two intermediate ones, and the bottom positions, which include foremen. With this division, it was possible to relate the three durations of decision to the four levels of management and to come out with useful quantifications about the amount of time involved in the course of decision at each level. In Figure III, the four levels of management are shown across the top, and at the left are the durations of decision—short, moderate, and distant.

Let us first compare the two extreme levels to learn about the essentials of the mental and moral demands on the decision-maker in the corporate hierarchy. At the lowest level of management (IV), 98 per cent of the decisions were of short duration, 96 per cent being

FIGURE III   THE MANAGEMENT OF TIME IN THE EXECUTIVE HIERARCHY
(Per Cent)

Duration of a Decision	Highest Level—I	Intermediate Level—II	Intermediate Level—III	Lowest Level—IV
Short				
Less than 1 week	3	37	58	96
1 to 2 weeks	0	17	10	2
Total	3	54	68	98
Moderate				
2 weeks-month	12	15	21	2
Over month to a year	35	27	9	0
Total	47	42	30	2
Distant—over a year	50	4	2	0
All durations	100	100	100	100

less than a week. Only 2 per cent were from one to two weeks and from over a month to a year. There are no decisions that involved more time than from two weeks to a month for the bottom grade of management.

At the highest level, half of the decisions took over a year to complete and over a third from four months to a year; 85 per cent of the decisions of top management endure so long that they do not overlap any of the decisions of lower management. Figure III can be examined in another perspective, the decisions that each man must make as he moves from one level to another. Most of the men were in lower positions earlier in their careers, when they had to make short-term decisions; yet they had to have the necessary capacity to control and relate themselves to the exacting demands of the immediate situation at that time, and in such a way that later they could move on up to the higher responsibilities that have longer time dimensions.

Let us now look at the sequence of events from the point of view of the man starting at the bottom. At level IV, 98 per cent of his decisions took less than a week. When he moved up to level III, 68 per cent took less than a week and under two weeks, but 30 per cent were moderate in duration and 2 per cent were over a year. He is promoted to level II, where over half of his decisions are still short-term; but 42 per cent are moderate and 4 per cent—double the last level—take over a year. Finally, he reaches a position of command at the top where only 3 per cent of his decisions are short-term, 35 per cent over a month to a year, and half take over a year before their outcomes are achieved.

Professor Martin summarizes all of his research on the factor of duration by saying, "decision situations at this top level are, there-fore, of a distant or remote focus. Under these conditions, the deci-sion maker must use the present instrumentally as a means to the future; his address to the problem must always have a forward ref-erence. Each succeeding, immediate present event must be viewed in terms of its consequences for sequential events to follow. In a sense, *the future must be brought into the manageable present*" (italics mine). In sum, as a man moves from the bottom to the top of the managerial status structure, long-term concepts are more often used. He must relate himself to himself and to others by long-term think-ing. There is an increasing need to act on abstractions about indirect relations, which are often remote from him, and about distant events rather than present ones. As his authority increases and his power becomes greater, they must be exercised on the basis of well-organ-ized facts, usually collected by a staff to whom he must be closely and realistically related. They, too, deal with him in terms of abstractions that he can analyze, act on, and make decisions with. As he moves up there is ever greater freedom of action but less certainty about the structure which he occupies and the meaning of the immediate events in terms of future consequences.

Ambiguity must forever be part of the world in which he must make decisions that have to be successful more often than not if he is to continue in his position or advance himself. There is greater need to make decisions with less objective control. There is con-stantly more individual risk-taking and need for the risk-taker to be sufficiently well in control of himself and the world around him to reduce the amount of error and randomness. In brief, there is in-creasing need for individual autonomy within the corporate hierarchy itself. Those who do not have autonomy, those who are supine, those without the ability to make decisions from within and hold to them by their own moral strength are rarely capable of staying in such positions. Men in such positions must structure and re-structure the world around them, or they necessarily must fail. Constantly they face greater and greater heterogeneity and are in need of greater and greater ability to handle themselves autonomously, mentally and morally, in the activities which their statuses demand. In brief, the moral and mental orders which they occupy demand the very kinds of personalities which are more often found among the top business leaders in the corporate structures of America.

THE ROLE OF HIGHER EDUCATION IN A FLUID SOCIETY
WITH OPEN STATUS

A large proportion of top corporate and government executives not only are mobile occupationally but have been mobile from their early origins. Many come from families very modestly placed. Moreover, the study of big-business leaders shows that there is greater fluidity now in the social structure and in the status structure; there is more mobility, except for farmers, from all lower levels than a generation ago. The society is clearly more flexible and more fluid. There is more opportunity for individuals in corporate enterprise to come from the bottom. Furthermore, fewer sons of the wealthy stay at the top of business than formerly. There is more circulation from the bottom to the top and more movement out of the top than previously. The top statuses of business and government are more open to competition. The principles of birth, still important and of real significance, do not operate as easily as previously. The basic values of our society, including that nebulous but all important belief in the American Dream, are more real now and less the stuff of legend and fiction than a generation ago.

The fluid world at the top of the corporation in today's rapidly changing emergent society demands a high percentage of autonomous men. The emergent future forever flows out of today's decisions, and these men must be such that they can allow the flow of such changes to continue. The competitive well-being of a corporation or a government agency requires that such men manage them today to make decisions for a manageable tomorrow. As might be supposed, the society itself necessarily has had to provide institutions by which men can be transformed from what they were born to and what they might expect from their families of birth and encouraged to move forward and upward into positions of command. This has been the function of increasing higher education for business and government leaders.

The role of higher education has had at least two fundamental functions in our contemporary society and in the emergence of the great community. It has transformed men for occupational mobility. Now, men move upward not so much because of early apprenticeship on the job but by their previous training in institutions of higher learning. Here they obtain the necessary preparation and the kinds of experiences which help them advance. The institutions of higher education also have been instruments of cultural conservation and rapid emergent change. From the great departments of science—social, biological, and physical—and from other disciplines, have come many of the new advances.

The proportion of big-business men with college degrees today, even these men now in their fifties, is very high. Three-fourths attended a university, 57 per cent graduated, one-third had some graduate study, and many had advanced degrees. These men had eight times more college training than men in the general population. Today, all top businessmen who were born to all occupational levels have more college education than the sons of big-business leaders in 1928! The proportions of federal executives with college degrees are still higher. Eighty-one per cent of the civilian federal executives have one or more university degrees, twelve times more than males in the general population.

The executives of large-scale, complex organizations, whether they be corporate, government, or otherwise, tend to prepare themselves and to gain the necessary requisites for advancement from early college training. Such men, more often than not, arrive at college with the necessary potentials for autonomous action. In college they can acquire the necessary skills and training to complete and develop the ability to make the decisions necessary for high command.

Executive autonomy with individual choice-making is necessary equipment for managers operating not only in the corporation but in the fluid world of today. The individual applies the rules as an individual to himself and others. The fact that he is autonomous does not mean that he is completely different and separate from his group; rather, it means that he has within him the intellectual and moral capacities to make the decisions necessary for immediate action in the great society.

As our society becomes more extended and more diverse, the areas of individual decision-making necessarily become more frequent, complex, and demanding. When the individual moves from status to status and from place to place he must, sometimes from moment to moment, redefine who he is and what he does primarily on his own initiative. One must suspect that rapid social change in the inner and outer worlds of everyone and greater social complexity increase the social need for individual decision-making, for intellectual and moral autonomy, and instigate our society's high evaluation of individuals with these capacities. Such people are not "organization men" but autonomous men.

We have continued to talk about autonomous leaders as individuals who quite early in their lives developed personalities capable of being trained sufficiently to advance to high position. Until now we have not examined the institution which is principally responsible for training and personality formation in this and other societies. We have spoken only in passing of the relation of the corporation to that most basic of all institutions, the family. It is now necessary to draw attention to the family, in terms of its functions for creating personalities adapted to present needs. We must also try to find out what it is, what it is doing in this new emergent world, in the great society where corporations and other complex hierarchical organizations are dominant, where the local community no longer operates in such a way that it buttresses and strengthens the private intimacies of family life.

THE AUTONOMOUS FAMILY AND CORPORATE CHANGE
IN THE FLUID SOCIETY

The American family, the principal matrix of personality formation, nurtures the individuals and protects their private lives from the increasing demands of the new heterogeneous society and helps readjust them to the emergent forms of its great complex organizations. Meanwhile, the families of each individual, those of birth and marriage, continue to change as part of the flow of time in the emergent process of the great society. The increasing technological control over the natural environment and the elaboration of the division of economic and social labor are connected closely with the family's external relations; the latter function, in many ways, in the development of the total system.

There is obviously a greater and greater need in our complex society for a family system so constituted that it can train children, not only for the new occupations that are continually developing and appearing, but also for living in the diverse changing economic and social systems. Such training cannot be for fixed and permanent tenure of individuals in one position; American families must train their children for individual decision-making, for movement, and for individual choice in a changing society by changing individuals. To allow men and women to move from occupation to occupation, and to leave one status and move into others, demands special training and the formation of persons capable, with minimal effort, of moving easily. This means adjustment, readjustment, and adjustment again. Such developments of the family system in our larger order of kindred are largely antithetical to what has previously prevailed and what is characteristic elsewhere. The *grosse familie* in many parts of Europe, of traditional China, and the earlier rather rigidly organized kinship system of nineteenth-century America are in sharp contrast to these free, semiautonomous family units. Management and corporate control in such societies, particularly succession between generations, function very differently than in America. There, one finds the family system interfering with free competition for higher status in the corporate structure; there, position may very well be fixed, so that no change of family position occurs between the generations—those at the top stay at the top and those at the bottom remain there. Fluidity of position can only exist where it is possible for the family to relate itself to an emergent society and where it can permit its individuals to be trained in such a way that they move from position to position and place to place without difficulty.

The continuing wider integration of corporate (occupational) statuses—extending horizontally over greater social and territorial

distances, more specialized occupations, and more diverse social con-
tacts—demands primary interaction by many corporate administrators
and others and is no longer confined to the local communities of
town and city. If located in one community, this kind of movement
often is from one suburb to another and to a kind of culture that is
different from the subculture out of which the individual has moved.
Accordingly, many families, motivated by diverse drives and goals,
journey from place to place to fill the available jobs. Money, improved status, better living conditions, and many other values drive
them as they move from status to status, from one suburb to another,
from town to town, and from region to region. The wider integration
of the heterogeneous occupational and social levels also extends over
more diverse vertical distances. Today, there are more positions at all
levels of prestige and power than yesterday. The recruitment of populations from below to fill positions above, and the loss of positions
from above, result in the continuous circulation of individuals and
families from level to level—while they may, perhaps at the same
time, be moving from place to place. All this, of course, is part of
the emergence of the one great society.

   To move easily, families cannot be too closely attached to their
kindred (extended kinship system) or they will be held to one
location, socially and economically maladapted. This is true both of
the family of birth and of the family of marriage. The same is true
for the individual moving from his family of parents and siblings over
to his family of marriage. Consequently, for structural congruence,
families of birth and marriage may be, and often are, loosely related.
One of the principal functions of the new family, now largely freed
from the group of kindred to the point where it can move autonomously, is to train autonomous individuals in sufficient numbers to
fill the needs of the society in which individuals must circulate and,
while doing so, make their own decisions. A strong hostility has been
growing toward the psychological dependency that is related to kinship control and the dominance of older generations. The definitions
of dependency, such as "immaturity," have increasingly become
"dirty words." One of the principal developing functions of the school
as it moves its control downward into the earlier years of the child

and upward into increasing maturity is to reinforce the development of individual autonomy and free the individual from too deep immersion in the demands of his kindred.

The movement through time of the American society partly consists of re-ordering older occupational and social statuses in the corporate and social structures. For this purpose, too, the family must train for flexibility in the person. Descent of occupation and training from father to son, and in proportion to the number of jobs available, is something that rarely occurs in the society. The loose family allows a new generation to change more adaptively, socially and personally, in a rapidly changing society. If the society is in equilibrium, change is not too difficult. If the society is in conflict and disfunctional, as it sometimes is, loose family organization is likely to reduce conflict because the emotional strain will not be felt as violently within the immediate group of intimate kindred. Loose family order provides greater maneuverability and flexibility both for the family and for the individuals who are members of it.

The increasing heterogeneity and wider integration of diverse groups, the development of individual moral autonomy, and autonomous families, partly freed from the restraints of the grandparental generation (which in most societies is powerful), have made the positions of older people weak. Grandparents exercise little, and sometimes no, influence upon their grandsons and granddaughters. Therefore, the traditions of the past have fewer opportunities to make their demands on the development of the new generations and to maintain and stabilize the traditional restraints. The effect on our culture of the reduction of the amount of control by the grandparental generation is probably almost incalculable.

The small autonomous family, freed of strong kinship ties, not only provides an ideal place for the training of autonomous persons in their formative period but later in their lives gives them the freedom to move in the highly fluid world of today.

The moving social equilibrium in America, involving not only harmonious and cohesive integrated change but varying degrees of disequilibrium, sometimes results in social conflict and personal disorder. Ordinarily, however, our society has moved toward increasing individuation and personal autonomy, with fluidity of status, without too much conflict. Still, anxiety and the need to know how to tolerate it in socially undefined situations are necessary parts of the equipment of most, particularly the men who lead the society in some of the complex organizations and, among these, particularly those of the rapidly changing corporate enterprises. The world around them is ambiguous and new; decisions must be made with insufficient evidence and with insufficient control. It is here that the autonomous person must function. It is for these places our society must be able to produce those who make the decisions necessary for our survival. In our kind of world, given its basic beliefs and its emergent character, we cannot continue advancing unless we are able to produce autonomous personalities.

One great society is now in being. The great corporations grow and expand. Big government extends itself enormously. Across the nation, primary, face-to-face interaction grows as the national community enters maturity; the future invades today, and each tomorrow advances the time of its arrival. Local communities are still important and still necessary parts of our social life, but instead of having their own autonomy, they are integral parts of the larger American— not to say world—social system. The changes occurring have developed one great society, a society which must continue to emerge and become something more than it is now.

The headwaters of the tumultuous, ever-present flood of this great society pour relentlessly forth. Seeming disorder is in them; chaos threatens. At not one but a thousand places open channels break through ancient self-imposed banks and strike forth in their own individual directions. In a multitude of freshets some rush heedlessly into nothingness, others spend their strength in stagnant pools to live in an eternity of stillness, while still others disappear in bleak sands that are bottomless, meaningless, and without form. In raging flux, new ideas, new values, new behaviors, and new personalities surge into the wide waters of the main stream; they beat themselves against its ancient sides and they struggle for positions of command at its central confluences; always they demand to grow, to expand and fulfill themselves. Yet the traditional banks of the great cultural stream, threatened forever with disaster, hold and constrain its deeper currents. Order confines disorder; chaos is not there. At each place in time all are transformed into the hard residues of the past, contributing their own fresh strength. Today's recent past holds the enormous power of ancient tradition and makes it part of the strength of the present. Thus, these deposits of collective experience are made ready to contain tomorrow's turbulence. We at this moment's flood tide often can know only disorder; but, tomorrow, others looking back will know and understand the present symmetries of our time, those contained in an order that far too often escapes our own fearful comprehension.